1

This book belongs to:

_____

Scorpio Daily Horoscope 2025

Author's Note: Time set to Coordinated Universal Time Zone (UT±0)

Contents

The 12 Zodiac Star Signs

2025

January

S	M	T	W	T	F	S
			1	2	3	4
5	6	7	8	9	10	11
12	13	14	15	16	17	18
19	20	21	22	23	24	25
26	27	28	29	30	31	

February

S	M	T	W	T	F	S
						1
2	3	4	5	6	7	8
9	10	11	12	13	14	15
16	17	18	19	20	21	22
23	24	25	26	27	28	

March

S	M	T	W	T	F	S
						1
2	3	4	5	6	7	8
9	10	11	12	13	14	15
16	17	18	19	20	21	22
23	24	25	26	27	28	29
30	31					

April

S	M	T	W	T	F	S
		1	2	3	4	5
6	7	8	9	10	11	12
13	14	15	16	17	18	19
20	21	22	23	24	25	26
27	28	29	30			

May

S	M	T	W	T	F	S
				1	2	3
4	5	6	7	8	9	10
11	12	13	14	15	16	17
18	19	20	21	22	23	24
25	26	27	28	29	30	31

June

S	M	T	W	T	F	S
1	2	3	4	5	6	7
8	9	10	11	12	13	14
15	16	17	18	19	20	21
22	23	24	25	26	27	28
29	30					

July

S	M	T	W	T	F	S
		1	2	3	4	5
6	7	8	9	10	11	12
13	14	15	16	17	18	19
20	21	22	23	24	25	26
27	28	29	30	31		

August

S	M	T	W	T	F	S
					1	2
3	4	5	6	7	8	9
10	11	12	13	14	15	16
17	18	19	20	21	22	23
24	25	26	27	28	29	30
31						

September

S	M	T	W	T	F	S
	1	2	3	4	5	6
7	8	9	10	11	12	13
14	15	16	17	18	19	20
21	22	23	24	25	26	27
28	29	30				

October

S	M	T	W	T	F	S
			1	2	3	4
5	6	7	8	9	10	11
12	13	14	15	16	17	18
19	20	21	22	23	24	25
26	27	28	29	30	31	

November

S	M	T	W	T	F	S
						1
2	3	4	5	6	7	8
9	10	11	12	13	14	15
16	17	18	19	20	21	22
23	24	25	26	27	28	29
30						

December

S	M	T	W	T	F	S
	1	2	3	4	5	6
7	8	9	10	11	12	13
14	15	16	17	18	19	20
21	22	23	24	25	26	27
28	29	30	31			

2025
Daily Horoscope

SCORPIO

As your astrologer, I wish to explain why one horoscope book may differ from another for each zodiac sign. The vast array of astrological activity constantly occurring in the sky requires me to focus on the essential aspect of the star sign I am writing for on any given day. Each zodiac sign is unique, and the various planetary factors affect them differently.

When crafting horoscopes, I pay special attention to the significant astrological aspects directly impacting a specific sign. By doing so, I can provide the most insightful and relevant guidance to individuals of that zodiac sign. While there might be multiple planetary alignments on a particular day, one aspect may hold more significance for a specific sign than others.

Considering the ruling planets and elements associated with each zodiac sign further refines my interpretations. This attention to detail ensures that the horoscope resonates with the distinct characteristics and tendencies of the star sign in question.

Ultimately, I aim to offer personalized insights and advice based on each zodiac sign's unique cosmic influences. By focusing on each star sign's most relevant astrological aspects, I can help readers better understand themselves and navigate the energies surrounding them. Embracing each zodiac sign's strengths, challenges, and opportunities allows me to create a horoscope book tailored to my readers' needs.

"We are born at a given moment, in a given place, and, like vintage years of wine, we have the qualities of the year and the season of which we are born. Astrology does not lay claim to anything more."

—Carl Jung

January

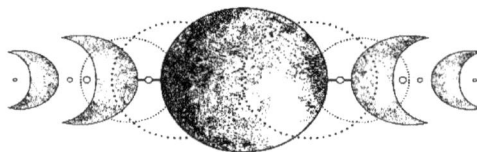

MOON MAGIC

Sun	Mon	Tue	Wed	Thu	Fri	Sat
			1	2	3	4
5	6	7	8	9	10	11
12	13	14	15	16	17	18
19	20	21	22	23	24	25
26	27	28	29	30	31	

New Moon

WOLF MOON

30 Monday

With the Moon's ingress into Capricorn and the arrival of the New Moon, you can focus on setting practical goals and working diligently to achieve them. The energy of Capricorn encourages you to progress toward your ambitions. Assess long-term plans and make necessary adjustments. Use this time to establish a solid foundation for endeavors and take steps toward manifesting dreams. Embrace the New Moon energy as a fresh start and a chance to create a path of success.

31 Tuesday

You soon create growth opportunities, build meaningful relationships, and experience a sense of community. This new chapter brings opportunities for self-discovery, creativity, and joy. A focus on personal growth draws positive change as a new path becomes more evident. Surrounding yourself with like-minded individuals opens the door to new possibilities. It helps you build meaningful relationships and create a supportive environment.

1 Wednesday

This New Year's Day, with the Moon ingress Aquarius, you may feel a strong sense of independence and individuality. The energy of Aquarius encourages you to break free from conventional patterns and explore new ideas and perspectives. It's an excellent opportunity to connect with like-minded individuals and engage in social activities that promote collaboration and innovation. You may feel drawn to causes that align with your values as you impact the world positively.

2 Thursday

Bask in the solar radiance as the sun traverses your wellness sector, illuminating the celestial path to holistic well-being. The cosmic spotlight invites you to prioritize self-care as a sacred ritual, a harmonious dance between body, mind, and soul. In the heavenly sanctuary of health, witness the transformative power of balance, where vitality flourishes. The universe also encourages your creativity as a celestial masterpiece, a testament to the divine artistry within your soul.

3 Friday

The Moon's ingress into Pisces enhances emotional sensitivity and intuition, encouraging trust in instincts and embracing your imaginative side. This aspect is a time for introspection and connecting with your spiritual essence. Nurture your emotional well-being and find solace in artistic and spiritual pursuits. Embrace the healing energy of Venus in Pisces, navigate any power dynamics with wisdom, and allow the gentle influence of the Moon in Pisces to offer inner peace.

4 Saturday

The Sun forms a sextile aspect with Saturn, presenting an opportunity to harness discipline, structure, and practicality. This alignment empowers you to take charge of your responsibilities and long-term goals. You can create a solid foundation for success by organizing your tasks, setting clear objectives, and following through with determination. It's an excellent time to establish healthy routines, honor commitments, and create steady progress.

5 Sunday

With the Moon entering Aries, you may feel energy and enthusiasm propelling you forward. This fiery and assertive influence encourages you to take decisive action and passionately pursue your passions. You are inspired to embrace new beginnings and assert your individuality. It's a time to trust your instincts and follow your gut feelings as you are more attuned to your needs. This lunar transit empowers you to take the lead, be proactive, and tackle challenges head-on.

6 Monday

With Mercury square Neptune, there is a potential for confusion and misunderstandings. It's essential to be mindful of misleading or unclear information and to double-check facts before making decisions. This aspect calls for heightened discernment and a critical eye to navigate through any illusions or misunderstandings that may arise. Embrace Mars's nurturing and intuitive energy in Cancer while maintaining a transparent approach to communication.

7 Tuesday

With the Moon entering Taurus, you may experience a heightened sense of stability and groundedness in your emotions. You seek comfort, security, and a sense of material well-being. This lunar influence encourages you to indulge in sensual pleasures and enjoy life's simple pleasures. You may find solace in creating a peaceful and harmonious environment around you, focusing on the beauty of nature and the tangible aspects of your surroundings.

8 Wednesday

With Mercury entering Capricorn, you can expect a shift in your thought processes. Your attention to detail and ability to analyze situations helps you make sound decisions. Take advantage of this time to set goals, devise strategies, and engage in meaningful discussions contributing to your long-term success. Your words carry weight and influence, so choose them wisely and use them to build a solid foundation for your plans and ambitions.

9 Thursday

The North Node, a guiding star on your cosmic journey, illuminates the path to your destined purpose. Trust the celestial compass as it points towards experiences and opportunities aligned with the trajectory of your soul. In the cosmic dance of fate, waltz confidently towards a purposeful life, where the North Node leads you to the grand finale of fulfillment. Embrace the electrifying currents of change, daring to traverse uncharted territories of thought.

10 Friday

With the Moon ingressing Gemini, your mind becomes active and agile, seeking new information and engaging in various mental activities. You may feel an increased desire to learn, read, and explore different ideas and perspectives. This transit is an excellent time to connect with others, exchange ideas, and expand your knowledge. Be open to new experiences and embrace the versatility of this lunar transit.

11 Saturday

Neptune's ethereal presence in your sector of friendships invites you to engage in a cosmic communion of shared dreams and ideals. Feel the celestial currents of empathy and creative inspiration flow through your social circles. Under Neptune's influence, cultivate connections that transcend the ordinary, allowing the divine waters to carry you to the shores of soulful camaraderie and collective imagination.

12 Sunday

As the Moon enters Cancer, you experience a heightened sensitivity and emotional depth. You become more attuned to your intuition and the needs of those around you. Your nurturing instincts are strong, and you seek comfort and security in familiar environments and with loved ones. This transit encourages you to prioritize self-care and emotional well-being, creating a nurturing space to recharge and find solace.

13 Monday

The combination of the Sun trine Uranus and the Full Moon invites you to embrace your authentic self, embrace change, and celebrate the achievements and growth that have brought you to this point. Trust your intuition, embrace your uniqueness, and allow the transformative energy of this period to propel you forward on your path of personal evolution. It is a time for reflection, letting go of what no longer serves, and embracing the lessons and blessings in your life.

14 Tuesday

With the Moon entering Leo and Venus forming a square with Jupiter, you enter a busy period filled with vibrant energy and expansive emotions. The Moon's ingress into Leo ignites passion, self-expression, and confidence. You are likely to feel a strong desire for recognition and appreciation, and your emotions are more likely to be expressed with flair and enthusiasm. Meanwhile, Venus square Jupiter brings abundance and indulgence to your relationships and desires.

15 Wednesday

The sun's radiant rays in your financial sector cast a celestial spotlight on abundance and material stability. Bask in the solar glow as the cosmic energy illuminates your financial landscape. Under the sun's influence, focus on cultivating a prosperous mindset and embracing the cosmic dance of economic well-being, allowing your material pursuits to flourish under the celestial rays. Let your spirit soar and embrace the cosmic adventure that unfolds.

16 Thursday

The Sun-opposed Mars aspect brings a clash of wills and a potential for conflict or power struggles. It's essential to be aware of your assertiveness and how you assert your desires, as it may create friction with others. This aspect can fuel a strong drive, but it's crucial to channel this energy constructively rather than engage in unnecessary conflicts. As the Moon moves into Virgo, you are encouraged to focus on the details, organization, and efficiency.

17 Friday

With the Sun sextile Neptune, you explore the realms of imagination, intuition, and spiritual connection. This harmonious aspect creates a flow between your conscious self and the ethereal energy of Neptune. It opens the door for creative inspiration, heightened sensitivity, and a deep sense of empathy. During this time, you may find that your intuition heightens, allowing you to tap into subtle energies and unseen forces.

18 Saturday

As Venus graces your sector of routines and well-being, the cosmic gardener tends to the garden of your daily existence. Feel the celestial petals unfurl as Venus encourages you to cultivate self-love and nourish your well-being. Under this astral horticulture, witness the blossoming of a radiant life where self-care becomes a cosmic ritual, and your daily routine becomes a celestial dance of balance.

19 Sunday

As Venus conjuncts Saturn, you may desire commitment in your relationships. This alignment brings stability and a craving for long-lasting connections. The Moon's ingress into Libra further enhances this focus on harmony and balance, urging you to seek fairness and cooperation in your interactions. With Mercury sextile Saturn and Mercury sextile Venus, your communication skills refine, allowing you to express your thoughts and feelings with clarity and diplomacy.

20 Monday

You are entering a cycle of increasing possibility. Being open to connecting with friends and sharing lively catch-ups draws a bonus into your social life. It offers a changing scene that nurtures stability and happiness as it brings grounded foundations that keep life engaging and vibrant. It brings an ambient environment that fosters harmony through the supportive conversations shared with kindred spirits.

21 Tuesday

With the Sun conjunct with Pluto, you may experience a powerful energy that brings intensity and transformation to your life. This aspect invites you to dive deep into your inner self, uncovering hidden truths and confronting fears or limitations. It encourages you to embrace personal empowerment and take charge of your life. As the Moon ingresses Scorpio, emotions intensify, and you may find yourself drawn to exploring the depths of your feelings.

22 Wednesday

With the red-hot influence of Mars blazing a celestial trail through your ninth house, the cosmic warrior invites you to embark on an odyssey of knowledge and exploration. You may sense the fiery passion of the red planet infusing your pursuits of higher learning and philosophical quests. Under the cosmic command of Mars, channel the dynamic energy into the pursuit of intellectual endeavors, daring to push the boundaries of your understanding.

23 Thursday

With Mercury trine Uranus, your mind is quick and open to new ideas and insights. This transit enhances your ability to think outside the box and find unique solutions to problems. It promotes intellectual stimulation, inventive thinking, and the potential for sudden breakthroughs. This aspect brings an energetic and dynamic influence, encouraging you to embrace change, think creatively, and be adaptable.

24 Friday

With the Moon's ingress into Sagittarius, you may feel a sense of expansion and a longing for freedom and adventure in your emotional landscape. This transit encourages you to embrace a more optimistic and open-minded approach to life. You may find yourself craving new experiences and a broader understanding of the world around you. It is a time to explore different beliefs, cultures, and philosophies that resonate with your inner truth.

25 Saturday

Venus trines Mars. You are in touch with your sensual side and will likely experience increased pleasure and enjoyment in your relationships and creative endeavors. This alignment supports healthy self-expression, confidence, and a proactive approach to pursuing your desires. Embrace the harmonious dance between Venus and Mars, allowing it to ignite your passions and inspire you to take bold and pleasurable actions in all areas of your life.

26 Sunday

Mercury sextile Neptune enhances your mental clarity and intuition. Your thoughts and ideas are infused with imagination and creativity, making it a suitable time for artistic and spiritual endeavors. You have a heightened ability to communicate your dreams and visions, and others are receptive to your ideas. This aspect encourages you to trust your instincts and tap into the deeper realms of your imagination.

27 Monday

Under the radiant glow of the Sun in your fourth house, the cosmic spotlight turns toward the foundations of your being and the sanctity of home and family. Feel the warmth of the solar energy infusing your domestic realm with vitality and clarity. In the heart of your inner sanctum, the celestial fire illuminates the contours of your emotional landscape, revealing the connections between self and surroundings. Bask in the solar brilliance as it casts a benevolent glow.

28 Tuesday

With Mercury ingress Aquarius, your thinking and communication take a more innovative and forward-thinking approach. You become intellectually stimulated and interested in exploring new ideas and concepts. Your mind is open to unconventional perspectives, and you may engage in stimulating conversations that challenge the status quo. This transit encourages you to embrace individuality and express your thoughts uniquely and creatively.

29 Wednesday

Aligned with the New Moon, this conjunction marks a time for beginnings and fresh starts. It is a time of setting intentions and planting seeds for future growth and transformation. The merging of Mercury and Pluto energies empowers you to dive into self-reflection, uncovering the subconscious patterns and beliefs that may be holding you back. It is a time to release what no longer serves you and embrace a more authentic and empowered way of expressing yourself.

30 Thursday

With Uranus turning direct, a wave of change and liberation sweeps through your life. This shift brings an awakening of individuality and a desire for freedom. You may feel an increased urge to break free from any constraints or limitations that have held you back. This transit is a time to embrace your unique quirks and authentic self. Embrace the unexpected and be open to innovative ideas and experiences that come your way.

FEBRUARY

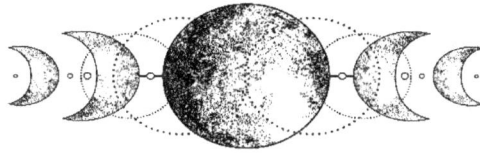

MOON MAGIC

Sun	Mon	Tue	Wed	Thu	Fri	Sat
						1
2	3	4	5	6	7	8
9	10	11	12	13	14	15
16	17	18	19	20	21	22
23	24	25	26	27	28	

NEW MOON

SNOW MOON

31 Friday

With the cosmic messenger Mercury gracing your fourth house, the celestial airwaves resonate with the delicate symphony of communication within the realms of home and family. Feel the gentle cadence of Mercury's influence as it encourages open dialogues and exchanges within the domestic sanctuary. Under this heavenly influence, your household becomes a cosmic hub of ideas and familial conversations, contributing unique perspectives.

1 Saturday

When Venus aligns with Neptune, it brings a touch of enchantment and romanticism to your world. This celestial dance inspires you to explore the depths of love, beauty, and imagination. You may find yourself drawn to artistic pursuits, seeking solace in music, art, or poetry. Your heart becomes attuned to the subtle nuances of emotions, allowing you to connect with others on a deeper level. It's a world of enchantment with no limits, and dreams have the power to manifest.

2 Sunday

With the Moon moving into Aries, you feel a surge of fiery energy and assertiveness within you. This ingress ignites your passion and drive, urging you to take bold steps and embrace new beginnings. You may feel a renewed sense of independence and a desire to assert your individuality. It's a time to be proactive, courageous, and assertive in pursuing your goals. The Aries Moon empowers you to take charge, make decisive choices, and enthusiastically go after what you want.

3 Monday

With Mercury forming a harmonious trine aspect to Jupiter, you discover a heightened intellect and expansive thinking. Your mind is sharp, and you can grasp complex concepts and see the bigger picture. This alignment brings optimism and a positive outlook, allowing you to approach situations with confidence and enthusiasm. Your communication skills are enhanced, making expressing your ideas and persuading others easier.

4 Tuesday

As Jupiter begins to move forward, the expansive energy amplifies, allowing you to move forward with greater clarity, optimism, and a renewed sense of purpose. It's a time to embrace your passions, take calculated risks, and trust in the abundance of opportunities that lie ahead. This cosmic alignment invites you to step into your power, embrace change, and make positive strides toward your goals and aspirations.

5 Wednesday

It's the perfect time for mapping out new goals. Expanding your life into unique areas offers a positive shift that attracts possibilities worth your time. Designing your life draws progression and aligns you towards achieving a positive result. A new attitude and rising confidence bring a chance to step out and enjoy growing a path that offers room to revolutionize the potential possible in your world. Focusing on stable and balanced foundations supports well-being and happiness.

6 Thursday

With the Moon moving into Gemini, you are entering a period of intellectual curiosity and heightened communication. Your mind becomes sharp and agile, ready to absorb new information and engage in stimulating conversations. This transit is a time to explore different perspectives and expand your knowledge in various areas of interest. You may find yourself seeking out social connections and engaging in lively discussions that broaden your horizons.

7 Friday

With Venus forming a harmonious sextile aspect to Pluto, transformative energy infuses your relationships and personal values. You experience deepening emotional connections and an intensified sense of passion and desire. This aspect brings forth the potential for profound and meaningful transformations in love, intimacy, and personal growth. You may find yourself drawn to exploring the depths of your emotions and forming bonds that profoundly impact your life.

8 Saturday

As the Moon moves into Cancer, you may notice a heightened sensitivity and emotional depth within yourself. Your intuition becomes more robust, guiding you toward a deeper understanding of your needs and those around you. You may find comfort and security in your life's familiar and nurturing aspects. This transit is an appropriate time to honor your emotions and create a safe space for self-care and self-nurturing.

9 Sunday

Mars trine Saturn. This alignment supports you in implementing practical strategies and making steady progress in your endeavors. It's a time of increased productivity and a sense of accomplishment as you channel your motivation into productive, structured activities. Trust your abilities and maximize this powerful alignment, which offers assertiveness, clarity, and disciplined action to move closer to your aspirations.

10 Monday

It's a time to bask in the spotlight, to let your personality radiate with charisma and warmth. Allow the Moon in Leo to ignite your passions, ignite your inner fire, and inspire you to live with playfulness and enthusiasm. Embrace this energy and let it leave a trail of inspiration and delight in your wake. Allow your emotions to guide you towards activities that bring you joy and fulfillment, and remember to embrace your authentic self as you navigate this vibrant lunar phase.

11 Tuesday

Embrace the opportunity to explore new possibilities and embrace your authentic self, even if it means stepping outside your comfort zone. Use today's cosmic energy to embrace innovation, adaptability, and the courage to follow your path, even if it diverges from societal norms. By embracing the Sun square Uranus aspect, you can harness its transformative power and embark on self-discovery and personal growth.

12 Wednesday

The Full Moon shines a light on emotions, bringing them to the surface for acknowledgment and release. It is a potent time for reflection, self-awareness, and gaining clarity on your desires and goals. You may feel a sense of heightened sensitivity and intuition during this phase, enabling you to gain insights and make empowered decisions. Use this time to celebrate your achievements, release what no longer serves you, and set intentions for the next lunar cycle.

13 Thursday

As the Moon moves into Virgo, it brings practical and analytical energy to your life. You may find yourself focused on organization, attention to detail, and seeking efficiency in your daily routines. This transit is a time to bring order and structure to your environment, as well as your thoughts and emotions. You may feel a strong desire to be of service to others, offering your skills and expertise in practical ways.

14 Friday

Mercury ingress Pisces is an excellent time to engage in heartfelt conversations, share your dreams, and connect with your loved ones. Pay attention to your intuition and trust the messages that come from within. This transit invites you to embrace the power of empathy and use it to strengthen your relationships and foster a sense of connection. Allow Pisces's loving and compassionate energy to guide your interactions and create meaningful and soulful harmonies.

15 Saturday

Moon ingress Libra. You may find yourself drawn to socializing, seeking companionship, and engaging in activities that promote harmony and cooperation. It's an excellent time to work on resolving conflicts and finding compromises that benefit everyone involved. Embrace Libra's diplomatic and charming energy as you navigate your interactions, aiming to create a sense of equilibrium and mutual understanding in your connections with others.

16 Sunday

A social aspect ahead kicks off a chapter that rejuvenates and renews your energy. It builds stable foundations around your home life that give you a chance to keep life secure and balanced. Indeed, getting back to basics and sharing with friends reduces stress levels; it opens a theme of improving circumstances that bring moments to treasure. It opens a self-expressive, joyful, and happy time spent with kindred spirits.

17 Monday

A social gathering becomes a focal point. It is a beautiful occasion that brings the opportunity to relax and engage with others. Sharing with friends lights the way forward towards expanding your life. You reveal a path that opens positive change as news arrives to bring a welcome boost. The wheels are in motion as new possibilities bring a burst of fresh air to your surroundings. Networking and mingling see you move in circles that offer expansion for your life.

18 Tuesday

As the Moon enters Scorpio, your emotions may deepen, bringing a sense of intensity and introspection to your inner world. You may probe beneath the surface and uncover hidden truths and motivations. It is a time for self-reflection and delving into the depths of your emotions, allowing yourself to embrace the transformative power of vulnerability. Simultaneously, with the Sun moving into Pisces, you may experience a heightened sense of compassion and empathy.

19 Wednesday

With the guiding hand of Jupiter in your financial sector, the cosmic philanthropist bestows the gifts of abundance and prosperity. The cosmic currents of economic optimism bring expansion as Jupiter's influence blesses your material realms. Under this benevolent celestial patronage, navigate the astral marketplace with confidence, attracting heavenly wealth and embracing the abundance that flows through your financial constellation.

20 Thursday

As the Moon enters Sagittarius and Mercury forms a square aspect with Jupiter, you crave adventure and intellectual curiosity. Sagittarius' expansive energy encourages you to seek new physical and intellectual horizons. You may strongly desire to broaden your knowledge, explore different cultures, or embark on a new educational journey. However, the square between Mercury and Jupiter reminds you to temper your enthusiasm with practicality.

21 Friday

Mercury's swift dance through your communication sector quickens the cosmic currents of intellectual expression. Feel the agile energy of the celestial messenger as it facilitates articulate conversations and seamless exchanges of ideas. Under Mercury's heavenly guidance, engage in thought-provoking dialogues, letting the astral winds carry your words to receptive minds, creating a celestial symphony of intellectual connection.

22 Saturday

Embrace the energy of Capricorn Moon's determination and resilience as you navigate challenges and strive for excellence. Use this period to organize your priorities, create a strategic plan, and take deliberate steps toward your desired outcomes. Remember to balance work and self-care, allowing yourself moments of rest and rejuvenation. By harnessing the practical energy of Capricorn, you can lay the groundwork for future success.

23 Sunday

A surprise invitation connects you with developing friendships; it emphasizes improving your social life. Friends and family link up to share news and communication with you. It sets off a lively pace for engaging with life as people reach out to offer support and kinship. Cheered on by rising prospects, you feel the wind beneath your wings, offering lightness and happiness. This supportive energy brings a considerable boost to your life.

24 Monday

As Mars turns direct, a surge of forward-moving energy ignites within you. After reflection and introspection, you are now ready to take action and make tangible progress in various areas of your life. This shift brings a renewed sense of motivation, drive, and assertiveness. You feel a powerful urge to push through obstacles, overcome challenges, and pursue your goals with vigor. Mars' direct motion empowers you to assert desires and boundaries and actively pursue goals.

25 Tuesday

It's a time to communicate clearly and concisely and seek practical solutions to any challenges. With the Moon in Aquarius and Mercury conjunct Saturn, you can think outside the box while grounding your thoughts in practicality and responsibility. Embrace this cosmic influence as it supports your intellectual pursuits and encourages you to contribute your unique perspective to the collective consciousness.

26 Wednesday

A new project arrives, and getting involved with this area lets you put your personal touch on things. Artistic expression and creativity are on the rise, opening pathways that grow your talents. A significant assignment boosts your spirit as it opens a clear path forward for your abilities. Working with your capabilities and developing life in new areas brings good fortune. It helps you create tangible results that guide a chapter of discovery and movement.

27 Thursday

Mercury's sextile Uranus sparks intellectual curiosity and a desire for new experiences and perspectives. You seek unconventional ideas and conversations that expand your mind. This aspect encourages you to embrace change, think outside the box, and express yourself uniquely and authentically. Take advantage of this dynamic cosmic energy to explore new concepts, connect with others on a deeper level, and embrace the magic of the unknown.

MARCH

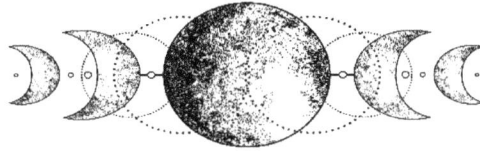

MOON MAGIC

Sun	Mon	Tue	Wed	Thu	Fri	Sat
						1
2	3	4	5	6	7	8
9	10	11	12	13	14	15
16	17	18	19	20	21	22
23	24	25	26	27	28	29
30	31					

New Moon

_____

_____

_____

_____

_____

_____

_____

_____

_____

_____

_____

_____

_____

_____

_____

_____

_____

_____

_____

Worm Moon

28 Friday

The energy of the New Moon supports you in manifesting your dreams and creating positive changes in your life. Embrace this moment to envision the future you wish to develop. Trust in your inner guidance and allow the energy of the New Moon to ignite your passion and motivation. This transit is a time of immense potential and possibility, and by harnessing the power of the New Moon, you can set the stage for a fulfilling and transformative journey ahead.

1 Saturday

As the Moon enters Aries, you feel a surge of energy and a renewed sense of vitality. This fiery and assertive energy ignites a passion within you, encouraging you to take bold actions and pursue your desires with courage. You're motivated to step out of your comfort zone and embrace challenges head-on. This lunar influence inspires you to be proactive and assertive in pursuing your dreams. It's a time to trust your instincts and take the lead in creating the life you envision.

2 Sunday

The Sun square Jupiter brings a need for balance and moderation. Be mindful of overindulgence or taking on too much, as the urge for expansion and growth needs to balance with practicality and discernment. Take this opportunity to review your beliefs and plans, making adjustments that align with your authentic self. Use the retrograde energy to delve into self-discovery, gain clarity in your relationships, and refine your communication style.

3 Monday

Mercury ingress Aries. Moon ingress Taurus. Emphasizing comfort, security, and the sensual pleasures of life, you may find solace in creating a cozy and nurturing environment. It's essential to balance your assertiveness and the need for peace, allowing your words and actions to align with your values and long-term goals. You can navigate this period with strength and grace by honoring your practical nature and expressing yourself authentically.

4 Tuesday

Within the depths of transformation and shared resources, Jupiter in Gemini adds a layer of intellectual exploration and communicative richness. Feel the expansive energy as Jupiter encourages an open-minded approach to shared assets and intimate connections. Under this celestial influence, delve into the mysteries of the eighth house with a curious and adaptable mindset. Jupiter invites you to explore the complexities of joint ventures and transformative experiences.

5 Wednesday

Moon ingress Gemini and Mercury's sextile Pluto aspect enhances your perception and intuition, allowing you to make meaningful connections and express yourself sincerely. It's an excellent time to engage in research, introspection, and soulful conversations that can bring transformation and empowerment. Harness the energy of the Moon in Gemini and the Mercury-Pluto sextile to embrace intellectual growth and embark on a journey of self-discovery.

6 Thursday

Incoming news brings an opportunity that bears fruit as you take steps toward building a venture that offers room to grow your life. As you dip into this new avenue of possibility, you discover kindred spirits who share similar goals. It brings a group environment that connects you with like-minded individuals who draw insightful discussions and supportive dialogues. There is some learning involved that opens life outwardly.

7 Friday

With the Moon transitioning into Cancer, you may find yourself experiencing a heightened emotional sensitivity and a deeper connection to your inner world. Your intuition becomes more pronounced, guiding you to nurture yourself and others with compassion and empathy. This lunar phase encourages you to create a safe and comforting environment where you can retreat and recharge. You feel more attuned to the needs of your loved ones, offering them emotional support.

8 Saturday

With the harmonious alignment of the Sun and Mars in a trine aspect, you can expect a boost of energy, motivation, and assertiveness. This dynamic combination empowers you to take decisive action and confidently pursue your goals. You'll feel a surge of vitality and enthusiasm, fueling your ambitions and inspiring you to step outside your comfort zone. You can make significant progress toward your objectives as your drive and determination amplify.

9 Sunday

Moon ingress Leo sees emotions take on a fiery and passionate quality, and you are eager to shine. Your warmth and generosity radiate, drawing others towards you. It's a time to embrace your inner joy, celebrate your individuality, and let your inner light shine brightly. Allow yourself to express your passions and pursue activities that bring you a sense of pleasure and fulfillment. Embrace Leo's playful and spirited energy, and let your authentic self take center stage.

10 Monday

You are on a continuous cycle of growth and revolution. Being open to change facilitates expansion as it opens life up to new options. It gives you the green light to link up with developing cutting-edge initiatives that deepen your knowledge. Actively exploring pathways around your life attracts new opportunities worth your time. It culminates in a turning point that cracks the code to grow your life outwardly.

11 Tuesday

Mercury conjunct Venus is a time to engage in heartfelt conversations, share your thoughts and ideas with gentleness and empathy, and seek out moments of beauty and harmony in your interactions. Allow this harmonious union of Mercury and Venus to inspire you to express your love and appreciation freely, fostering deeper connections and nurturing the bonds that matter most to you. Let the power of words and the beauty of your expression positively impact those around you.

12 Wednesday

When the Moon enters Virgo and the Sun forms a conjunction with Saturn, you have a time of practicality, discipline, and self-reflection. Your focus shifts toward efficiency, organization, and attending to the details of your life. You feel a strong sense of responsibility and a desire to establish order and structure in various areas. This alignment encourages you to assess your goals, set realistic expectations, and work diligently toward achieving them.

13 Thursday

With Mars in Cancer gracing your ninth house, the cosmic warrior infuses your quest for knowledge and exploration with emotional zeal. Feel the assertive energy as Mars encourages you to pursue intellectual adventures and broaden your horizons passionately. Under this celestial influence, your journey becomes a dynamic quest for emotional and intellectual growth. Mars invites you to explore territories of higher learning and philosophical exploration assertively.

14 Friday

During the Full Moon phase, coupled with the Sun's sextile aspect to Uranus and the Moon's ingress into Libra, you may experience rising awareness and a desire for greater harmony and balance. This celestial alignment encourages you to embrace change and embrace your unique individuality. The Full Moon illuminates emotions, giving you insight into relationships. It's a time to evaluate your connections and find ways to foster greater equality and cooperation.

15 Saturday

As Mercury turns retrograde, it invites you to enter a period of reflection and introspection. This celestial phenomenon encourages you to slow down and reassess various aspects of your life. It's a time to review your thoughts, communication patterns, and plans, ensuring they align with your true intentions. Take this opportunity to revisit unfinished projects, tie up loose ends, and address any miscommunications or unresolved issues.

16 Sunday

In the domain of partnerships and relationships, Neptune casts its mystical spell in your seventh house. Feel the cosmic enchantment as it weaves through the threads of connection, infusing your relationships with compassion, empathy, and otherworldly understanding. Under Neptune's celestial influence, partnerships become a dance of spiritual connection, where the boundaries between self and other dissolve in the cosmic waters of unconditional love.

17 Monday

Moon ingress Scorpio. It's important to honor and acknowledge your emotions during this period, even if they seem uncomfortable. Dive into the depths of your psyche and confront any buried feelings or unresolved issues. It is a time for personal growth and self-discovery, where you can let go of what no longer serves and embrace your authentic self. Trust the process and allow the transformative energy of Scorpio to guide you to greater self-awareness and empowerment.

18 Tuesday

With Mars energizing your career sector, the cosmic warrior ignites a resilient flame of ambition and determination. Feel the pulsating energy of Martian influence propelling you towards professional conquests and achievements. Under the celestial battle cry, seize the cosmic reins of your career path, conquer challenges with tenacity, and assert your heavenly presence in the professional arena.

19 Wednesday

Moon ingress Sagittarius and Sun conjunct Neptune is a time to let go of limitations and allow your intuition to guide a journey of self-discovery. Embrace the boundless possibilities that lie ahead and trust in the power of your dreams. This period will connect with your higher purpose and tap into a more profound sense of meaning and inspiration. Allow the energy of Sagittarius and the influence of Neptune to expand your consciousness and open life to new realms.

20 Thursday

A new chapter begins as the Sun enters Aries and marks the Vernal Equinox with the vibrant energy of spring; it brings new beginnings. Aries, the first sign of the zodiac, ignites an inner fire, inspiring you to take bold actions and enthusiastically pursue your passions. It's a time of self-discovery and empowerment where you can make an impact. The Equinox symbolizes a balance between light and darkness, reminding you to find harmony within yourself and your surroundings.

21 Friday

When Venus forms a sextile aspect with Pluto, powerful and transformative energy infuses your relationships and personal connections. It's a unique opportunity to delve deep into emotions, intimacy, and passion. This alignment encourages you to explore the hidden depths of your desires and confront any underlying fears or insecurities that may hold you back from experiencing profound connections. It is a time to embrace vulnerability and authenticity.

22 Saturday

When the Moon ingresses Capricorn, there is a shift towards more grounded and practical emotional energy. You may prioritize responsibilities, set ambitious goals, and focus on long-term plans. This lunar transit encourages you to take a structured and disciplined approach to your emotions and inner world. You may feel more determined, resilient, and capable of handling challenges. It's a time to nurture a sense of stability, organization, and self-control.

23 Sunday

When the Sun is conjunct with Venus and the Sun is sextile with Pluto, you experience a potent combination of passion, intensity, and transformative energy. This alignment brings a powerful magnetism to your personal relationships and creative endeavors. You draw experiences that ignite your inner desires and allow you to express your true self authentically. It is a time of heightened self-confidence as you radiate magnetic energy that attracts deep connections.

24 Monday

When the Moon ingresses Aquarius and the Sun conjuncts Mercury, you may experience a period of intellectual stimulation and a heightened sense of curiosity. Aquarius is an air sign known for its innovative and independent nature, while the Sun-Mercury conjunction amplifies mental clarity and communication. During this time, you may find yourself drawn to unique ideas, unconventional thinking, and engaging in meaningful conversations with others.

25 Tuesday

Mercury sextile Pluto alignment encourages you to explore topics of depth and significance, seeking to uncover hidden layers of meaning and exposing the underlying dynamics at play. Your communication style may profoundly impact you, as you can express your thoughts and ideas persuasively and convincingly. This aspect invites you to embrace the power of knowledge, engage in transformative conversations, and use your insights to create positive change.

26 Wednesday

Moon ingress Pisces is a time to engage in self-care and introspection, nurturing your soul and connecting with your innermost desires. Trust the whispers of your intuition and follow the gentle flow of inspiration that arises. Embrace the healing power of music, art, and any activities that bring you solace and tranquility. Allow yourself to dive into the depths of your emotions, embracing the mystery and magic of life.

27 Thursday

As the Black Moon moves into Scorpio and Venus enters Pisces, profound and mysterious energy envelops your being. This cosmic alignment invites you to explore the depths of your desires, passions, and unconscious realms. The conjunction of Venus and Neptune enhances your ability to experience love, beauty, and artistry on a transcendent level. You may draw spiritual connections and romantic experiences that touch your soul.

28 Friday

Moon ingress Aries. It's a time to be proactive, make decisions, and initiate projects that align with your authentic self. Allow the pioneering spirit of Aries to propel you forward and inspire you to take charge of your life. Trust your instincts, embrace spontaneity, and fearlessly venture into uncharted territories. The Moon in Aries empowers you to embrace your inner warrior and embark on self-discovery and personal growth.

29 Saturday

As the darkened Moon aligns with the Sun, you are encouraged to reflect on your goals, dreams, and aspirations. This aspect is a fertile period for planting the seeds of your desires and initiating new projects or endeavors. Trust your intuition and listen closely to the whispers of your heart, as they hold the keys to your true passions. Embrace the energy of the New Moon as a blank canvas, where you can paint your intentions and envision the life you wish to create.

30 Sunday

Embrace the gentle whispers of your soul and let your imagination guide you toward new possibilities. As the Moon settles into Taurus, you find stability and comfort in connecting with the sensual pleasures of life. Take this opportunity to nourish your body and senses and find solace in the beauty of the physical world. By harmonizing your dreams and intuition with the practicality of the earthly realm, you can navigate this transitional phase with grace and purpose.

April

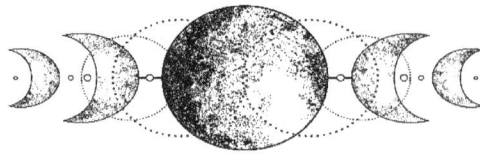

MOON MAGIC

Sun	Mon	Tue	Wed	Thu	Fri	Sat
		1	2	3	4	5
6	7	8	9	10	11	12
13	14	15	16	17	18	19
20	21	22	23	24	25	26
27	28	29	30			

NEW MOON

PINK MOON

31 Monday

Life ahead supports your efforts to improve circumstances. A busy time of socializing promotes stable foundations that cultivate thoughtful discussions. It has you feeling in sync with others who link with you to share thoughtful discussions. Sharing thoughts within your circle brings insight into the path ahead. It opens the floodgates towards advancement as it pears you up with opportunities that head towards growth.

1 Tuesday

As the Moon enters Gemini, you may feel a shift in your mental energy and communication style. This transit ignites your intellectual pursuits and encourages you to engage in stimulating conversations and explore ideas. Your mind becomes curious, adaptable, and eager to explore new concepts and connect with others intellectually. It is a time of heightened mental activity, where you may engage in lively conversations, absorb further information, and express your thoughts easily.

2 Wednesday

Change is swirling around your career life. A compelling journey ahead draws remarkable results. It lets you gain traction in developing your dreams. It corresponds with planning, gathering intel, and having all the resources required to advance life. You stake your claim in an ambitious area that captures the essence of excitement. It has you feeling optimistic about possibilities, giving you the green light forward.

3 Thursday

Moon ingress Cancer is a time to prioritize self-care and emotional well-being. You may find comfort in spending time with loved ones, creating a cozy sanctuary at home, or indulging in relaxing activities that replenish your soul. Allow yourself to honor your emotions and seek the solace you need during this lunar phase. Trust your instincts, listen to your heart, and embrace the loving energy that Cancer brings forth.

4 Friday

With Saturn sextile Uranus and Mars sextile Uranus, you may experience a harmonious blend of stability and innovation. This aspect encourages you to balance tradition and progress, allowing you to make positive changes while staying grounded. You are empowered to take calculated risks and explore new territories with confidence. The energy of Uranus stimulates your desire for freedom and uniqueness, while Saturn provides structure and discipline.

5 Saturday

With Mars forming a trine aspect to Saturn, you may find a harmonious balance between action and discipline in your life. This alignment empowers you to channel your energy and drive in a focused and structured way, allowing you to progress steadily toward your goals. You have the strength and determination to tackle challenges and overcome obstacles with a strategic and patient approach. Trust in your abilities and that your efforts will yield fruitful outcomes.

6 Sunday

As the Moon enters Leo, you may feel heightened confidence and self-expression. The Sun's harmonious sextile with Jupiter further amplifies this expansive energy, filling you with optimism and a belief in your abilities. You are encouraged to step outside your comfort zone and explore new opportunities for growth and success. The Venus trine Mars aspect also brings a harmonious blend of passion and harmony to your relationships and creative endeavors.

7 Monday

Your thinking becomes sharper, and you regain a sense of momentum in your thoughts and ideas. Take advantage of this energy to resolve any lingering issues, communicate your thoughts clearly, and regain a sense of forward motion. Trust your instincts, stay grounded in practicality, and let the combined influence of Venus conjunct Saturn and Mercury guide you towards more stable and productive experiences in your relationships and communication endeavors.

8 Tuesday

You may find satisfaction in tackling tasks, analyzing situations, and seeking routine efficiency. Embrace the harmonious energy of Venus and Uranus, which encourages you to explore new possibilities and embrace the unexpected while grounding yourself in the practicality and discernment of the Virgo Moon. This combination supports you in finding a balance between excitement and stability, fostering growth and personal development in various aspects of your life.

9 Wednesday

Good news ahead brings heightened security that offers a grounded and balanced environment in your working life. Current constraints lift, enabling you to plot a course toward advancement. You open an upward trend in your working life that sees sunny skies emerging overhead. It lets you release the worries as it dials down the stress and enables you to get busy in a productive environment that offers rising prospects.

10 Thursday

Your career heads toward growth as an upswing of potential lets you step out on a journey that expands your talents. It offers a fruitful time for working with your abilities as you find progression occurs quickly during this time. As you gain traction on developing your goals, you discover your situation is evolving, broadening your reach and enabling you to climb the ladder toward success. Deepening your knowledge offers impressive results.

11 Friday

As the Moon enters Libra, you may seek balance, harmony, and a sense of fairness in your interactions and surroundings. This lunar transit invites you to consider the needs and perspectives of others while maintaining your sense of self. You may feel a heightened desire for peace and cooperation, valuing diplomacy and compromise in your relationships. This aspect is an excellent time to engage in activities that promote beauty, art, and social connections.

12 Saturday

The North Node's guiding light in your sector of personal development directs your focus toward individual evolution and self-discovery. Trust the cosmic compass as it points the way through the celestial labyrinth of self-realization. In the cosmic unfolding of your destiny, follow the North Node's guiding light toward a deeper understanding of your unique essence, where the dance of personal growth harmonizes with the symphony of your soul.

13 Sunday

During the Full Moon, you may experience intensified emotions and heightened awareness. As the Moon moves into Scorpio, you can explore the depths of your emotions and tap into your inner strength and resilience. It's a time for introspection, transformation, and embracing the mysteries of life. Trust your instincts and allow the powerful energy of this celestial alignment to guide you on a journey of self-discovery and empowerment.

14 Monday

In the domain of daily routines and well-being, the Sun in Aries adds a touch of flair and excitement to your approach to health and work. Embrace a spirited and dynamic attitude toward your well-being, finding joy in active pursuits and bold choices. The Sun encourages you to take the lead in matters of health and work, infusing your daily routines with the assertive energy of Aries. This celestial alignment invites you to embrace the thrill of a healthy and vibrant lifestyle.

15 Tuesday

You crack the code to a brighter phase when information crosses your path, drawing excitement. It allows you to flex your talents and use your abilities in a progressive arena. Advancing your skills by incorporating innovative techniques enables you to achieve a successful result. The pressure eases as you light up pathways of growth and prosperity. Success is on the horizon, seeing inspiration surging in your world.

16 Wednesday

Today's combination of the Moon in Sagittarius and Mercury in Aries brings a dynamic and enthusiastic energy to your intellectual pursuits. It encourages you to boldly pursue your passions, speak your truth, and embark on exciting academic endeavors that align with your authentic self. Embrace this cosmic influence and let your curiosity lead the way as you navigate the vast landscapes of knowledge and self-expression.

17 Thursday

When Mercury forms a conjunction with Neptune, it brings dreamy and intuitive energy to your thoughts and communication. Your mind becomes more attuned to the subtle realms, imagination, and spiritual insights. You may find yourself drawn to artistic or creative endeavors, expressing yourself through poetry, music, or visual arts. This conjunction enhances your intuition and ability to pick up on unspoken messages and underlying emotions in conversations.

18 Friday

The combination of Mars in Leo and the Moon in Capricorn empowers you to be bold while maintaining a steady and responsible demeanor. You are motivated to achieve greatness and leave a lasting impact on the world around you. Trust your abilities, harness your inner strength, and channel your energy towards accomplishing your ambitions. Success awaits as you embrace the dynamic power of Mars in Leo and the grounded influence of the Moon in Capricorn.

19 Saturday

Sun ingress Taurus. Mars trine Neptune alignment infuses your actions with a compassionate and intuitive touch, allowing you to pursue your dreams and desires with a harmonious blend of ambition and inspiration. Trust in the power of your imagination and tap into your inner wisdom to manifest your aspirations. The Sun in Taurus and the Mars trine Neptune aspect provide a fertile ground to create a fulfilling life aligned with your true purpose.

20 Sunday

With the Moon's ingress into Aquarius, you feel a shift in your emotional landscape, embracing freedom and individuality. This cosmic combination encourages you to embrace your unique qualities, connect with like-minded individuals, and embrace a spirit of innovation and progressive thinking. Allow yourself to celebrate this Easter Sunday with a sense of liberation, intellectual curiosity, and the joy of unexpected connections.

21 Monday

Sun square Mars aspect encourages mindfulness of actions and reactions, as impulsive decisions may lead to unnecessary conflicts or obstacles. By harnessing the powerful energy of Mars and aligning it with the vitality of the Sun, you can navigate these challenges and transform them into opportunities for growth and achievement. Remember to exercise self-control, choose battles wisely, and direct your energy towards endeavors that align with your true desires and purpose.

22 Tuesday

Life leads to a fantastic time that expands the boundaries of your life. It gives room to cultivate a new interest and dabble in hobbies that promote well-being and happiness. Many raw potentials are ready to connect you with a circle of like-minded individuals. It illustrates what you can achieve by staying open to change and exploring the broader world of potential outside your door. Lightness and momentum carry you forward.

23 Wednesday

As the Moon gracefully enters Pisces, it brings a sense of sensitivity and introspection to your emotional landscape. You may find yourself deeply attuned to your intuition and emotions, navigating the realms of dreams, imagination, and compassion. However, the Sun square Pluto adds a touch of intensity to the atmosphere. It calls for your attention to personal power, transformation, and potential inner conflicts.

24 Thursday

A cheerful chapter ahead grows your social life. It shines a light on a stabilizing environment that contributes to rock-solid foundations in your world. From this stable basis, you get involved with group projects and join forces with others who offer creative insights and ideas into areas worth developing. It lets you sink your teeth into a journey that channels your abilities into growing an exciting enterprise.

25 Friday

As Venus aligns with Saturn in conjunction, it brings a serious and grounded energy to your relationships and a sense of beauty. You may feel a more substantial need for stability and commitment in your interactions with others, seeking deeper connections built on trust and responsibility. Meanwhile, with the Moon moving into Aries, you're infused with a fiery and assertive spirit, ready to take charge and pursue your desires.

26 Saturday

Improving your circumstances brings a gentle flow of abundance into your personal life. It offers a positive influence that promotes a brighter, more connected way forward in your life. Changes ahead nourish this environment and provide thoughtful discussions that encourage bonding. It kicks off a time of progress and growth as you discover you have all the right ingredients to add spice to your romantic life.

27 Sunday

With the Moon entering Taurus and the occurrence of a New Moon, you have an opportunity for fresh beginnings and setting intentions related to stability, security, and sensual pleasures. This cosmic interplay is a time to ground, focus on practical matters, and nurture your physical and emotional well-being. Embrace the nurturing energy of Taurus and use the transformative power of the Mars-Pluto opposition to release any toxic patterns or behaviors that hinder your growth.

MAY

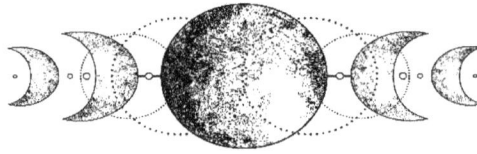

MOON MAGIC

Sun	Mon	Tue	Wed	Thu	Fri	Sat
				1	2	3
4	5	6	7	8	9	10
11	12	13	14	15	16	17
18	19	20	21	22	23	24
25	26	27	28	29	30	31

NEW MOON

FLOWER MOON

28 Monday

A change ahead helps release past issues that stalled progress in your life. News arrives that delivers exciting possibilities as it offers room to mingle and connect with your social life more often. A mix of manifestations at your disposal helps brew a refreshing time to expand your circle. Mingling with others draws fresh ideas as possibilities bounce around in an engaging atmosphere. You open a social chapter that brings a shift forward, leading to a wellspring of abundance.

29 Tuesday

Moon ingress Gemini is a good time for learning, networking, and engaging in social interactions that expand your knowledge and broaden your horizons. Embrace the energy of Gemini's mutable nature, allowing yourself to flow with the changing currents of information and ideas. This transit offers you the chance to embrace mental agility, connect with others on an intellectual level, and indulge your curiosity in various areas of interest.

30 Wednesday

Venus ingress Aries. This transit encourages you to embrace spontaneity and take bold action in love, creativity, and self-expression. It's a time to ignite passion and fearlessly pursue your heart's desires. Embrace the warrior energy of Aries, and let your true desires and inner fire guide your actions and intentions. Remember to stay true to yourself as you embark on this exciting new chapter, embracing the spark of Venus in Aries.

1 Thursday

You may be more attuned to your intuition and find solace in creating a peaceful and harmonious environment around you. It is a time to honor your emotional needs and prioritize self-care and self-nurturing. You may seek the company of loved ones or create a cozy sanctuary where you can retreat and recharge. Allow the gentle and compassionate energy of Cancer Moon to nourish and listen to the whispers of your heart as you navigate the ebb and flow of your emotions.

MAY

2 Friday

Venus conjunct Neptune. This alignment encourages you to embrace love's power and let your intuition guide your interactions and choices. It's a time to indulge in the enchanting qualities of life, seeking inspiration from nature, music, and the ethereal realms. Allow Venus and Neptune to weave their magic, reminding you of the profound interconnectedness of all things and the limitless possibilities within your heart and soul.

3 Saturday

Moon ingress Leo. Use this time to engage in activities that please you and allow your authentic self to shine through. Embrace your individuality and let your creative spirit soar as you radiate warmth and charisma to those around you. Remember to balance your need for attention with genuine generosity and appreciation for others, as this lunar energy encourages a heartfelt connection and celebration of your unique gifts and the talents of those you encounter.

4 Sunday

As Pluto turns retrograde, you may feel a subtle but powerful shift in the depths of your being. This celestial event invites you to dive inward and explore the hidden realms of your psyche. It's a time of introspection and transformation, where you can confront and release deep-seated fears or attachments that no longer serve you. You might find yourself drawn to delve into the mysteries of life, seeking a deeper understanding of your motivations and desires.

MAY

5 Monday

The combination of Mercury sextile Jupiter and the Moon in Virgo empowers you to make logical and informed decisions while encouraging you to explore new possibilities and embrace a growth-oriented mindset. It's an excellent time to expand your knowledge, engage in meaningful conversations, and refine your skills. Trust in your intellect and intuition as you navigate this phase, and embrace the opportunities for personal and intellectual growth that come your way.

6 Tuesday

Venus's sextile Pluto aspect encourages you to explore the depths of your desires and connect with others on a soulful level. It's a good time for deepening emotional bonds, healing relationship wounds, and experiencing profound transformation through love and intimacy. You may also find that your creative expression heightens, allowing you to tap into your artistic talents and channel your emotions into artistic endeavors.

7 Wednesday

The seventh house becomes a stage where the enduring qualities of Taurus take center stage in your interactions with others. The Sun encourages you to approach relationships with patience and a focus on building lasting connections. Embrace the cosmic warmth of the Sun as it bathes your partnerships in the grounded and enduring energies of Taurus, fostering a sense of security and appreciation for the tangible bonds that connect you with others.

8 Thursday

Moon ingress Libra. During this time, you have an opportunity to enhance your diplomatic skills and find ways to bring more equilibrium into your personal and professional interactions. Embrace the energy of Libra and strive to find common ground and mutual understanding in your relationships. By cultivating a sense of harmony and balance, you can create a more peaceful and fulfilling environment for yourself and those around you.

9 Friday

In the cosmic realm of partnerships and relationships, Uranus in Taurus brings a revolutionary wave of change and unpredictability. Feel the electric currents as Uranus urges you to redefine your approach to one-on-one connections. Under this celestial influence, relationships become dynamic collaborations that push the boundaries of tradition and challenge established norms. Uranus encourages the spirit of innovation, fostering an environment where each individual thrives.

10 Saturday

Mercury ingress Taurus. Moon ingress Scorpio. You may find yourself delving into your innermost feelings and desires, seeking emotional depth and authenticity. You may also experience a heightened intuition and a passion for emotional connection on a profound level. Allow this combination of Mercury in Taurus and the Moon in Scorpio to guide you toward a deeper understanding of yourself and the world around you.

11 Sunday

With Mercury positioned in Taurus in your seventh house on Mother's Day, the cosmic communicator adds a touch of steadiness and depth to your interactions with your mother or mother figures. Conversations take on a thoughtful and considerate tone, revolving around the dynamics of your relationship and the shared values that bind you together. Mercury in Taurus encourages expressions of love and fosters an atmosphere of mutual understanding and appreciation.

12 Monday

During the Full Moon, you may experience heightened emotions and a sense of illumination. It's a time of culmination and release, with intense and transformative energy. However, the square between Mercury and Pluto adds a layer of intensity to your communication and thought processes. You may engage in deep conversations or experience power struggles in your interactions. This aspect can bring strong opinions and a desire to uncover hidden truths.

13 Tuesday

As the Moon moves into Sagittarius, you may feel a sense of adventure and expansion. This lunar transit encourages you to embrace a more optimistic and open-minded approach to life. You may feel renewed curiosity and a longing to broaden your horizons. This transit is an ideal time to engage in activities that expand your knowledge and perspective, such as travel, learning, or connecting with different cultures and philosophies.

14 Wednesday

In the domain of daily routines, Venus in Aries adds a touch of flair to your approach to health and work. Embrace a spirited and dynamic attitude toward your well-being, finding joy in active pursuits and bold choices. Venus encourages you to appreciate taking charge of your daily routines, infusing them with the assertive energy of Aries. This celestial alignment invites you to find value in pursuing activities that bring passion to your work and health practices.

15 Thursday

Moon ingress Capricorn is a time to assess your ambitions and set realistic plans. The Capricorn influence encourages you to be diligent, patient, and resourceful. It's a good time for organizing your priorities, working towards your aspirations, and nurturing a sense of personal achievement. Embrace the determined and determined nature of Capricorn as you navigate your emotional landscape during this lunar transit.

16 Friday

The borders of your world open and draw a refreshing time shared with friends. You unlock a vibrant atmosphere that grows your world in a supportive direction. Sharing time with friends rejuvenates your energy and restores equilibrium. It offers grounded foundations that promote balance and harmony. You get in touch with a more playful side of life as fun and friendship take prominence. You enjoy a light-hearted journey shared with friends as you broaden your horizons.

17 Saturday

The Sun's radiant energy and Uranus' revolutionary influence can ignite individuality and innovation. Embrace this cosmic alignment as an invitation to embrace your true self, express your authentic voice, and take bold steps toward your growth and liberation. Be open to the unexpected and be willing to adapt to the shifting circumstances around you. Trust your intuition and allow your inner light to guide you on this exciting journey of self-discovery and transformation.

18 Sunday

When Mercury forms a square aspect with Mars, it can create dynamic and potentially challenging energy in your communication and mental pursuits. With the Moon's ingress into Aquarius, you may feel a heightened sense of independence and a desire to break free from conventional thinking. Embrace your unique perspective and use it to inspire innovative ideas and solutions. It is a time to think outside the box and embrace your individuality.

19 Monday

A new journey is ready to begin your life. News arrives, which offers an opportunity for growth. It opens a positive trend that helps you make tracks toward developing an exciting area worth your time. Advancement is imminent, and you can build a pleasing result by being open to new possibilities that cross your path. It is an ideal time to explore nurturing new areas and extend your reach into progressing a curious assignment that comes calling.

20 Tuesday

When the Sun forms a sextile aspect with Saturn, it brings stability, discipline, and ambition. You may feel a strong sense of purpose and a desire to structure your goals and tasks efficiently. This aspect supports your efforts to establish a solid foundation and work toward long-term success. With the Moon entering Pisces, your emotional sensitivity and intuition heighten. It's a time to tune into your inner world and focus on your dreams, creativity, and spiritual pursuits.

21 Wednesday

Cosmic undercurrents may leave you feeling unsettled and restless. This uneasy vibe is a sign to look for new leads, as gaining insight into the path ahead will provide you with a valuable gateway. It is to your benefit to generate new leads and advance your skills. Against what has been an unsettling backdrop, you soon expand your life and move towards developing a new endeavor. Your limitless imagination enables new ideas to spring to life.

22 Thursday

Venus forms a harmonious trine aspect with Mars, creating a beautiful synergy between passion and harmony in your life. You may experience a harmonious balance between your desires and your ability to take action. This aspect enhances your charisma, magnetism, and attractiveness, making it a good time for social interactions and romantic pursuits. With the Sun forming a supportive sextile with Neptune, it brings a touch of inspiration and spirituality to your day.

23 Friday

News arrives that opens pathways in your social life. It brings an invitation to your door that enables you to connect in a community environment. Mingling with others draws new people into your circle of friends. It opens a time that expands your life, bringing a changing scene on the horizon. This dynamic environment leaves you feeling optimistic about future possibilities. It lights a way towards abundance and happiness.

24 Saturday

With Mercury aligning with Uranus, your mind electrifies with innovative and original ideas. This aspect encourages you to think outside the box, embrace unconventional thinking, and seek intellectual stimulation. You may experience flashes of insight and sudden breakthroughs in your communication and thought processes. It's a time to embrace change, embrace your unique perspective, and explore new ways of expressing yourself.

25 Sunday

When Saturn enters Aries, it shifts your approach to personal responsibility and discipline. This transit encourages you to take charge of your life, set clear boundaries, and take a structured and organized system to achieve your goals. You may find yourself more self-disciplined and focused on long-term planning and success. This period invites you to confront any fears or limitations that may hold you back and develop a strong sense of self-reliance and independence.

MAY

26 Monday

As Mercury enters Gemini, your communication skills and mental agility heighten. You'll find yourself more inclined to engage in intellectual pursuits, connect with others through meaningful conversations, and express your ideas with clarity and precision. With Mercury forming a sextile aspect to Saturn, your thinking becomes more disciplined and focused, allowing you to approach tasks and projects with a practical mindset.

27 Tuesday

New Moon. As Mercury forms a trine aspect with Pluto, your mind fills with profound insights and the power to delve deep into the hidden truths and mysteries. This alignment sparks intellectual curiosity and empowers you to communicate your ideas with authority and conviction. Your words hold influence, and you can persuade and inspire others. This transit is a potent time for self-reflection, introspection, and exploring the depths of your psyche.

28 Wednesday

As the Moon moves into the nurturing and sensitive sign of Cancer, you may discover a more meditative and emotionally focused state. This lunar ingress invites you to connect with your inner world, your emotions, and the needs of your heart. It's a time to honor and nurture yourself, seeking comfort and security in your surroundings. You may desire emotional connection with loved ones and a need to create a sense of home and belonging.

29 Thursday

In the depths of transformation and shared resources, the Sun in Gemini shines its light on the mysteries of the eighth house. Your approach to intimate connections and joint ventures becomes intellectually charged and adaptable, reflecting the transformative energy of Gemini. Embrace the joy of delving into the complexities of shared experiences, finding satisfaction in the exploration of profound ideas and shared intellectual pursuits.

JUNE

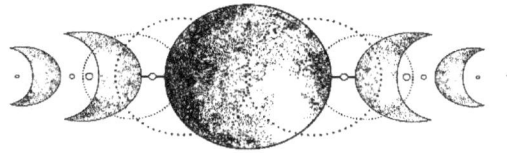

MOON MAGIC

Sun	Mon	Tue	Wed	Thu	Fri	Sat
1	2	3	4	5	6	7
8	9	10	11	12	13	14
15	16	17	18	19	20	21
22	23	24	25	26	27	28
29	30					

New Moon

STRAWBERRY MOON

30 Friday

When the Sun aligns with Mercury, your mind becomes sharp and focused, allowing you to express yourself with confidence and clarity. Your thoughts and communication are infused with vitality and passion, making it a great time to share your ideas and engage in meaningful conversations. With the Moon moving into Leo, you'll experience a boost of creative energy and a desire to shine brightly. It is a time for self-expression, creative pursuits, and stepping into the spotlight.

31 Saturday

As planetary energies undergo the end-of-month shift, a period of cosmic recalibration emerges. This introspective phase urges you to review and reassess your communication styles and thought processes. Embrace the potential for personal growth and a deeper understanding of your mental landscape as the celestial dance takes on a reflective rhythm. A subtle realignment of energies prompts an exploration of self-awareness.

1 Sunday

Within the cosmic energies prevailing today, there's a dynamic interplay, fostering a harmonious blend of assertiveness and affection. This celestial dance invites you to embrace the vibrant currents around you, encouraging heartfelt interactions and pursuit of desires infused with enthusiasm. A balance of fiery passion and harmonious connections shapes the atmosphere, enabling you to navigate your day with a spirited and loving approach.

2 Monday

You can embrace a practical and detail-oriented approach as the Moon moves into Virgo. This transit is a time for focusing on organization, efficiency, and taking care of the finer details in your life. You will likely feel a sense of purpose and a desire to improve your routines and daily habits. Use this energy to analyze your tasks and responsibilities, seeking ways to streamline and enhance your productivity.

3 Tuesday

Indications from celestial alignments unveil a powerful convergence, marking a time of significant transformation and disciplined expansion. This cosmic synchrony invites you to set ambitious goals while maintaining a grounded approach, fostering long-term success and enduring growth. The celestial arrangement encourages you to find equilibrium between expansion and structure in your endeavors, navigating your path with purpose.

4 Wednesday

As the Moon enters Libra, you may find yourself drawn to cultivating harmony, balance, and harmony in your relationships and surroundings. You have a heightened awareness of the needs and perspectives of others, making it easier for you to empathize and find common ground in your interactions. This ingress is a good time for fostering peace and cooperation, whether in personal relationships, friendships, or professional collaborations.

5 Thursday

With Mercury sextile Mars, your communication skills and mental agility heighten. This aspect fuels your drive, determination, and assertiveness, enabling you to express yourself clearly and confidently. It's an excellent time for taking action, making decisions, and initiating new projects. Your words carry power, and your ability to think quickly on your feet can help you overcome challenges and achieve your goals.

6 Friday

Venus ingress Taurus. Your desires may focus on creating a harmonious and balanced environment in your relationships and surroundings. Take time to indulge in self-care and pampering, allowing yourself to enjoy the present moment fully. With Venus in Taurus, you can find greater contentment and fulfillment by embracing sensual pleasures and cultivating a sense of beauty and harmony. Use this time to nurture your desires and build a strong relationship foundation.

7 Saturday

When the Moon ingresses Scorpio, it brings intensity and depth to your emotional landscape. You may find yourself delving into the mysterious realms of your inner world, seeking to uncover hidden truths and understand the deeper layers of your psyche. This transit invites you to embrace your emotional intensity and dive fearlessly into the depths of your feelings. It's a time of transformation and rebirth as you release old emotional patterns and emerge more empowered.

8 Sunday

You may find yourself drawn to nurturing conversations and seeking emotional connection in your interactions. It's a good time for learning, studying, and exploring subjects that ignite your curiosity and bring you a sense of emotional fulfillment. The alignment of Mercury and Jupiter in Cancer opens up possibilities for personal growth and expanded consciousness. Embrace the transformative power of knowledge and emotional connection as you navigate this phase.

9 Monday

When Mercury squares Saturn, you may encounter challenges or obstacles in your communication and thought processes. It could feel like there are limitations or restrictions in expressing yourself or gaining clarity. However, remember that obstacles can also be opportunities for growth and learning. The Moon's ingress into Sagittarius brings a sense of adventure and expansion to your emotions. You may seek new experiences and broader horizons.

10 Tuesday

In the unfolding cosmic dance, celestial bodies weave a tapestry of innovation and bold initiatives. A dynamic conjunction propels the atmosphere with a desire for change and the courage to break free from limitations. Embrace the unexpected opportunities arising from this celestial choreography, allowing the cosmic dance to propel you toward exciting and groundbreaking ventures. The planetary movements invite you to step into a realm of transformative energies.

11 Wednesday

Full Moon. Mercury sextile Venus. During a Full Moon, you may experience heightened emotions and a culmination of energies. It's a time of release and illumination, where you can gain clarity and insights into various aspects of your life. With Mercury sextile Venus, there is a harmonious flow between your thoughts and your social interactions. Your communication skills are enhanced, allowing you to express your feelings and ideas with charm and diplomacy.

12 Thursday

When the Moon ingresses Capricorn, you may feel a sense of determination and responsibility taking hold. There is a focus on practicality and structure, urging you to prioritize your goals and progress steadily. This energy supports your ambition and encourages you to take a disciplined approach to your endeavors. You may find yourself more focused on long-term success and willing to make the necessary effort to achieve your objectives.

13 Friday

Within the cosmic script of Friday the 13th, the cosmic forces inscribe a day of mystery and cosmic resonance. The energies align to create an ambiance where the ordinary meets the extraordinary, prompting you to embrace the cosmic enigma with an open heart and an adventurous spirit. Embrace the cosmic script of this day, allowing the mysteries to unfold and guide you toward a unique and transformative experience.

14 Saturday

As the Moon enters Aquarius, you may feel a sense of independence and a desire for greater personal freedom. Aquarius energy encourages you to embrace your uniqueness and express your individuality. You may find yourself drawn to unconventional ideas and innovative approaches. This transit is a time to explore new perspectives as your emotional focus may shift towards the collective, and you may feel a stronger sense of belonging to a larger community.

15 Sunday

When Mars squares Uranus and Jupiter squares Saturn, you may experience a tension between the need for change and the desire for stability. This combination can bring about a sense of restlessness and a craving for freedom and independence. You may seek to break free from limitations and pursue your individuality. Still, at the same time, there might be challenges and responsibilities that require careful planning and patience.

16 Monday

Moon ingress Pisces. Pisces is a watery, dreamy sign encouraging you to connect with your emotions. You may feel more compassionate, empathetic, and attuned to the needs of others. It is a time to trust your instincts and listen to the subtle whispers of your inner voice. Your imagination and creativity heighten, allowing you to tap into a rich source of inspiration. Creating a nurturing and peaceful environment for yourself during this lunar transition is essential.

17 Tuesday

Mars ingress Virgo. You may feel the cosmic urge to take care of practical matters, attend to your physical well-being, and streamline your daily life. Harness the energy of Mars in Virgo to bring structure and order to your endeavors. Pay attention to the small details and strive for excellence in all that you do. By channeling this energy effectively, you can accomplish great things and make significant progress toward your goals.

18 Wednesday

Moon ingress Aries. Aries is a fiery and assertive sign known for its passion and drive. During this time, you are encouraged to take initiative, be bold, and embrace new beginnings. You might feel more confident and ready to take on challenges or pursue your goals enthusiastically. It's a favorable period for asserting yourself, starting new projects, and taking decisive action. Trust your instincts and embrace your inner warrior spirit.

19 Thursday

When Jupiter squares Neptune, you may experience a clash between idealism and reality. This aspect can bring about a sense of disillusionment or confusion, as your dreams and aspirations may be at odds with the practicalities of life. It's essential to be mindful of potential illusions, unrealistic expectations, or over-idealizing situations or people. You may find yourself grappling with uncertainty or questioning your beliefs and philosophies.

20 Friday

In the intricate tapestry of the cosmos, the energies interlace to create a vibrant fusion of influences. This cosmic interweaving suggests a harmonious blend of resilience and receptivity. Embrace the nuanced energies surrounding you, allowing the cosmic tapestry to guide you toward a balanced and adaptable approach. The celestial currents gently prompt you to navigate your experiences with a sense of equilibrium, fostering a journey filled with strength and openness.

21 Saturday

The energy of Taurus reminds you to slow down, appreciate the beauty around you, and indulge in sensory experiences that nourish your soul. With the Sun in Cancer, you are encouraged to explore your emotional depths and deepen your connections with loved ones. It is a time for reflection, renewal, and setting intentions for the coming season. Embrace the nurturing energy of Taurus and Cancer as you create a harmonious and fulfilling season ahead.

22 Sunday

With Mars forming a harmonious sextile to Jupiter and the Sun in a challenging square aspect to Saturn, you navigate a dynamic and somewhat contradictory energy. On the one hand, the Mars-Jupiter sextile brings confidence, enthusiasm, and a desire for expansion. You feel motivated and driven to take action toward your goals and aspirations. However, the Sun's Square to Saturn introduces a dose of realism and potential obstacles.

23 Monday

With the Moon transitioning into Gemini, you may feel a sense of restlessness and curiosity. This cosmic shift encourages mental stimulation and a desire for intellectual exploration. However, the Sun's square aspect to Neptune brings a subtle undertone of confusion and uncertainty. It's essential to be mindful of potential illusions, delusions, or unrealistic expectations that may cloud your judgment during this time.

24 Tuesday

Sun conjunct Jupiter. You are encouraged to step outside your comfort zone and embrace the adventure that awaits you. With the Sun's vitality and Jupiter's wisdom on your side, you can adopt a brighter and more expansive version of yourself, ready to seize the opportunities that come your way. Trust your abilities, embrace the positive energy, and let the Sun-Jupiter conjunction illuminate your path toward personal and professional fulfillment.

25 Wednesday

With the Moon entering Cancer and marking a New Moon, you are entering a phase of emotional renewal and fresh beginnings. This lunar energy encourages you to nurture your inner world, tap into your intuition, and set intentions for the future. The New Moon in Cancer invites you to connect with your emotions, create a sense of emotional security, and strengthen your relationships with loved ones. It's a time to cultivate self-care and find comfort in the familiar.

26 Thursday

The Sun-Mars sextile fuels your motivation and drive, empowering you to take action and pursue your goals with determination. As Mercury enters Leo, your communication style becomes bold and expressive. You can captivate others with your words and convey your ideas with passion. Embrace this energy and let your creativity shine. This cosmic transit is a time to assert yourself, embrace individuality, and express thoughts with your voice.

27 Friday

Moon ingress Leo lunar phase ignites your sense of playfulness and encourages you to embrace joy and celebration. Channel your inner lion and step into the spotlight with courage and grace. Let the Leo Moon inspire you to express yourself fully and embrace the limitless possibilities. It's time to let your inner fire burn bright and enjoy the magic of being uniquely you. Embody the qualities of generosity, warmth, and enthusiasm as you embark on creative exploration.

28 Saturday

Mercury trine Saturn. Mercury trine Neptune. It is a favorable time for spiritual pursuits, artistic endeavors, and deepening your connection with the mystical aspects of life. With Mercury's harmonious aspects to Saturn and Neptune, you have no trouble balancing practicality, intuition, intellect, and spirituality. Your thoughts and words profoundly impact you, allowing you to communicate with clarity, depth, and a touch of magic.

29 Sunday

The opposition between Mercury and Pluto brings about a clash between reason and deep-rooted emotions. It can stir up power struggles or challenges in communication and decision-making. Your mind may seek to delve into the depths of complex matters, seeking hidden truths and uncovering underlying motivations. Meanwhile, the Moon's ingress into Virgo enhances your analytical and practical nature.

JULY

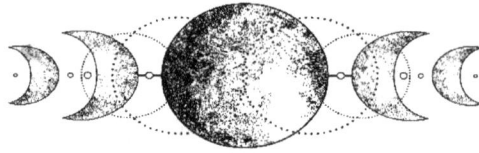

MOON MAGIC

Sun	Mon	Tue	Wed	Thu	Fri	Sat
		1	2	3	4	5
6	7	8	9	10	11	12
13	14	15	16	17	18	19
20	21	22	23	24	25	26
27	28	29	30	31		

ESCORPIO

NEW MOON

BUCK MOON

30 Monday

With the Sun illuminating your ninth house, the cosmic luminary infuses your quest for knowledge and exploration with a nurturing and emotionally rich energy. Your approach to intellectual pursuits becomes deeply connected to your sense of emotional security and familial values. Embrace the joy of expanding your horizons with those you hold dear, finding fulfillment in the exploration of meaningful ideas and shared experiences.

1 Tuesday

Moon ingress Libra. You will likely be more diplomatic and tactful in your communication, aiming to find fair and equitable solutions to disagreements. Being mindful of your needs and boundaries ensures you maintain a healthy balance between giving and receiving in your relationships. Use this time to foster cooperation, compromise, and a sense of fairness in your interactions with others, creating a harmonious and pleasant atmosphere in your personal and social life.

2 Wednesday

Aligned planetary forces prompt a focus on practicality and discipline within the cosmic tapestry. The harmonious alignment encourages methodical thinking and structured communication, creating a foundation for effective decision-making and strategic planning. Embrace the grounded energies at play, navigating your endeavors with clarity and a tangible approach that aligns with the harmonious celestial arrangement.

3 Thursday

You are guided under the influence of a powerful alignment. The energies converge to facilitate spiritual growth and transformation. This harmonious interweaving encourages you to embrace the mystical currents permeating your life, guiding you toward a deeper understanding of your higher purpose. Engage with the unseen forces shaping your journey, allowing the celestial guidance to illuminate the path to spiritual enlightenment and personal growth.

4 Friday

As Venus moves into Gemini, you may seek variety and intellectual stimulation in your connections. It's a favorable time for socializing, networking, and engaging in activities that promote camaraderie and collaboration. Your social interactions become more lively and diverse, allowing for exploring different ideas and perspectives. With Neptune turning retrograde, it's a period for introspection and reflection. You seek a deeper understanding of dreams and intuitions.

5 Saturday

Within the celestial tapestry, subtle energetic shifts radiate, inviting a transformative dance between cosmic forces. This infusion of energies encourages you to remain attuned to the subtle vibrations surrounding your experience. Embrace the dynamic interplay of celestial forces, fostering an awareness that allows you to navigate your day with heightened intuition and a sense of alignment with the cosmic currents.

6 Sunday

When Venus forms a sextile aspect with Saturn, your relationships and creative endeavors may offer stability, dedication, and a sense of long-term commitment. This harmonious alignment brings practical and grounded energy to matters of the heart, allowing you to build solid foundations and make wise choices in your interactions. Simultaneously, the sextile between Venus and Neptune adds a touch of magic and inspiration to your experiences.

7 Monday

Uranus enters Gemini, and a fresh wave of innovative and intellectual energy sweeps into your life. This transit encourages you to embrace change, explore new ideas, and engage in stimulating conversations. You may find yourself drawn to unconventional approaches and unique perspectives, fueling your curiosity and inspiring you to think outside the box. As Venus forms a trine with Pluto, powerful transformational energy is in your relationships and personal values.

8 Tuesday

In today's cosmic dance, there is a graceful interplay of energies, inviting you to engage with the rhythm of the universe. The celestial ballet encourages a harmonious blend of intuition and action, urging you to trust the unseen forces guiding your path. Embrace the dynamic choreography of cosmic energies, allowing your steps to be driven by a blend of heavenly wisdom and your innate instincts.

9 Wednesday

Moon ingress Capricorn transit encourages you to focus on your responsibilities, goals, and long-term ambitions. It's a time to take a structured and disciplined approach to your tasks, progress steadily, and set realistic expectations. Use this time to assess your long-term objectives and take practical actions that align with your aspirations. The Capricorn influence helps you tap into your inner resilience and determination, allowing you to tackle challenges calmly and composedly.

10 Thursday

The Full Moon invites you to celebrate your achievements, acknowledge your growth, and express gratitude for the blessings in your life. It's an opportunity to tune into your inner wisdom and intuition, trusting that the path ahead will align with your highest good. Embrace the transformative energy of the Full Moon and allow it to guide you toward greater self-awareness and personal fulfillment. Trust and surrender to the cosmic powers and embrace the Full Moon's expansion.

11 Friday

Moon ingress Aquarius. Embrace individuality and let your authentic self shine. It is a time to explore new possibilities, challenge the status quo, and contribute your unique voice to collective endeavors. Embrace the energy of Aquarius and let it inspire you to think outside the box, connect with others on a deeper level, and make a positive impact in your community. Trust your intuition, embrace your eccentricities, and let your inner rebel guide you toward new horizons.

12 Saturday

Within the celestial currents, a gentle influence unfolds, bestowing a sense of tranquility and emotional resonance. This cosmic breeze encourages you to pause and reflect, allowing your emotions to guide your actions. Embrace the quiet moments, and let the gentle celestial influence shape your experiences. Engage with the expansive energies, inviting a sense of curiosity and discovery to shape your journey in alignment with the cosmic flow.

13 Sunday

Saturn turns retrograde—Moon ingress Pisces. During this time, you may find yourself more attuned to your dreams, intuition, and spiritual insights. Use this phase to connect with your inner wisdom, nurture your emotional well-being, and dive into creative and imaginative pursuits. Trust in the process of self-reflection and allow yourself to flow with the intuitive currents that guide you toward a greater understanding of yourself and your path.

14 Monday

With the Sun illuminating Cancer in your ninth house, the cosmic explorer within you is driven by a deep emotional connection to knowledge and higher learning. Your approach to your career involves a continuous journey of discovery, where each endeavor becomes an opportunity for personal and intellectual growth. The Sun in this placement encourages you to infuse your career with a sense of purpose and meaning, exploring paths that align with your emotional truth.

15 Tuesday

Today's celestial alignments indicate a harmonious convergence, creating a landscape conducive to synergy and collaboration. This cosmic harmony encourages cooperative endeavors and shared visions. Embrace the interconnected energies at play, allowing the celestial alignments to guide you toward meaningful connections and collaborative ventures. Embrace the transformative currents guiding you towards greater harmony.

16 Wednesday

When the Moon enters Aries, you may feel a surge of energy and motivation. Your emotions become more fiery and assertive, pushing you to take action and pursue your goals with determination. It is a time to embrace your independence and assert your individuality. You might feel a strong need for self-expression and maintaining your needs and desires. Trust your instincts and follow your passion as you navigate this dynamic and energetic period.

17 Thursday

Within the cosmic script, the astrological landscape weaves a narrative of influence and potential. The celestial signatures inscribed in the cosmic canvas suggest a story of subtle shifts and cosmic nuances. Embrace the unfolding tale written in the heavenly language, allowing the astrological landscape to guide your interpretations and actions, inviting you to dance harmoniously with the celestial threads that shape your stellar narrative.

18 Friday

As Mercury turns retrograde, you may experience a shift in your communication and thought processes. It's a time to review and reflect on your ideas, relationships, and plans. The retrograde period invites you to slow down, pay attention to details, and reassess your strategies. With the Moon entering Taurus, there is a grounding and stabilizing influence that helps you approach situations with patience and practicality.

19 Saturday

Within the cosmic script of your domestic space, the astrological landscape weaves a narrative of influence and potential. The celestial signatures inscribed in the cosmic canvas suggest a story of harmony within your home. Embrace the unfolding tale written in your destiny, allowing the astrological landscape to guide your interpretations and actions in your journey, inviting you to dance harmoniously with the celestial threads that shape your home narrative.

20 Sunday

Moon ingress Gemini. Use this energy to expand your knowledge, connect with like-minded individuals, and express yourself clearly and wit. Embrace Gemini's versatility and flexibility, allowing yourself to embrace different perspectives and adapt to changing circumstances. You may find that teamwork and collaboration lead to more positive outcomes. This lunar transit encourages you to embrace curiosity and engage in stimulating activities that nourish your intellect.

21 Monday

Within the harmonious cosmic frequencies in the workplace, a suggestion emerges, inviting you to cultivate a balanced and dynamic approach to your professional life. This cosmic alignment encourages a rhythmic flow of collaboration and individual contribution. Embrace the nuanced interplay of celestial forces within your career, navigating your workday with awareness of the harmonious dance orchestrating the cosmic symphony in your journey.

22 Tuesday

As the Moon moves into Cancer and the Sun enters Leo, you may feel a shift in your emotional landscape and a renewed sense of self-expression. Cancer's nurturing and intuitive energy focuses on your emotional well-being and the need for comfort and security. It's a time to tune into your feelings and nurture yourself and those around you. The Sun in Leo shines a light on your unique qualities and encourages you to embrace individuality.

23 Wednesday

As the Sun forms a harmonious sextile with Uranus, you can embrace the energy of change and innovation in your life. This cosmic aspect encourages you to explore new ideas, take risks, and break free from old patterns. It's a time to embrace your unique individuality and express yourself authentically. The Venus square Mars aspect brings a dynamic tension between love and desire, creating a passionate and potentially challenging energy.

24 Thursday

The Sun trine Neptune enhances intuition and imagination, allowing you to tap into your spiritual and creative energies. It's a time to connect with your dreams, trust your intuition, and explore the deeper dimensions of your soul. With the New Moon, a fresh cycle begins, offering you an opportunity for new beginnings, setting intentions, and manifesting your desires. It is a powerful time to align your heart's desires with practical action as you embark on self-discovery and growth.

25 Friday

Sun opposed Pluto. This opposition urges you to confront your fears, shadows, and hidden desires, inviting you to shed old patterns and embrace personal growth. It's a time for self-reflection, inner work, and releasing what no longer serves you. Be courageous in facing your inner demons, and allow the transformative energy of this aspect to guide you towards personal empowerment and rebirth. Approach challenges with honesty, integrity, and self-awareness.

26 Saturday

When the Moon ingresses Virgo, you may seek practicality, organization, and attention to detail in your daily life. This energy encourages you to focus on the small tasks and responsibilities that contribute to your overall well-being and efficiency. You may feel satisfied in accomplishing tasks and finding practical solutions to problems. This period can also enhance your ability to analyze situations objectively and offer helpful advice to others.

27 Sunday

Celestial frequencies in your social haven beckon, creating an atmosphere of gentle allure and shared experiences. This cosmic alignment encourages you to open your home to social interactions, fostering a sense of community and togetherness. Embrace the nuanced interplay of celestial forces within your living space, navigating your social interactions with a heightened awareness of the harmonious dance orchestrating the cosmic symphony in your home.

28 Monday

As you navigate the transformative cosmic currents in your career, there is a suggestion of dynamic shifts and growth energies. The celestial dance encourages you to approach your professional endeavors with an open mind and a willingness to adapt. Embrace the transformative energies at play, allowing them to guide you towards innovative solutions and a harmonious alignment with your career trajectory.

29 Tuesday

Moon ingress Libra encourages you to consider different perspectives and find common ground with those around you. It is an excellent time to communicate openly and find compromises that promote mutual growth and support. Embrace this period as an opportunity to cultivate meaningful connections and encourage peace and equilibrium. Use this period to strengthen your relationships with others and boost a sense of peace and harmony in your personal and social life.

30 Wednesday

In the realm of your work life, subtle energies beckon you to infuse your professional pursuits with creativity and authenticity. The celestial ballet invites you to immerse yourself in the inspired vibrations that surround your career path. Embrace the harmonious dance of cosmic forces within your work environment, allowing their ethereal touch to guide you towards moments of professional insight and innovative breakthroughs.

31 Thursday

Venus ingress Cancer and Sun conjunct Mercury configurations hint at subtle shifts and transformative potential in your career landscape. These cosmic whispers suggest a narrative of growth and evolution in your professional endeavors. Engage with the hints presented by the celestial configurations, allowing their guidance to enhance your understanding and connection with the cosmic energies that shape your work life.

AUGUST

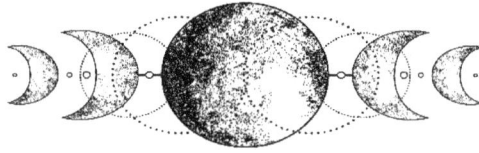

MOON MAGIC

Sun	Mon	Tue	Wed	Thu	Fri	Sat
					1	2
3	4	5	6	7	8	9
10	11	12	13	14	15	16
17	18	19	20	21	22	23
24	25	26	27	28	29	30
31						

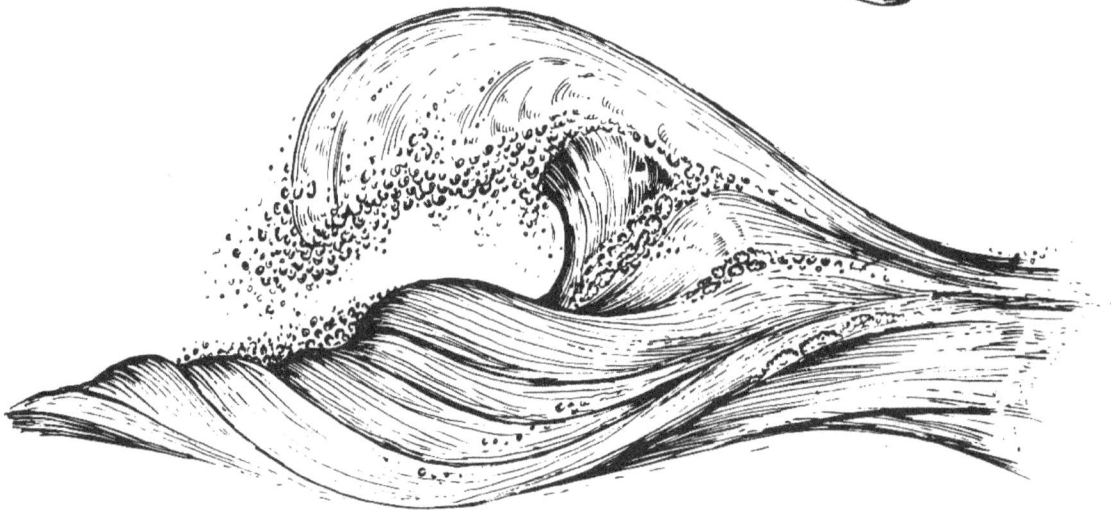

NEW MOON

STURGEON MOON

AUGUST

1 Friday

Venus square Saturn. Venus square Neptune. You may find it challenging to see things clearly and discern between genuine emotions and idealized fantasies. It's essential to stay grounded and realistic during this period, taking time to assess your relationships and emotional boundaries carefully. With introspection and a willingness to face reality, you can navigate these challenges and find more authentic and fulfilling connections in the long run.

2 Saturday

The cosmic dance suggests a blend of vibrant connections and nurturing atmospheres. The celestial ballet invites you to infuse your home space with warmth and friendly vibrations. Embrace the harmonious dance of cosmic forces within your domestic sphere, allowing their ethereal touch to guide you toward moments of familial connection and shared joy. You enjoy shared moments of love, understanding, and support within your domestic haven.

3 Sunday

As the Moon enters Sagittarius, you may feel a sense of adventure and curiosity taking center stage in your emotions. This cosmic shift encourages you to seek new experiences, broaden your horizons, and embrace a more optimistic outlook. You might find yourself drawn to activities that involve travel, learning, or exploring different cultures. This transit is a time to embrace spontaneity and let your adventurous spirit guide you.

4 Monday

The regal Sun in Leo graces your tenth house, enhancing your career and public image with a magnetic aura. You are driven to achieve recognition and success in your professional life, often taking on leadership roles with natural authority. A desire for admiration and acknowledgment of your talents fuels your ambition. It's essential to balance your need for recognition with humility and to use your influence to inspire and uplift those around you.

5 Tuesday

Moon ingress Capricorn transit encourages you to focus on your long-term goals and take steps towards achieving them. You might feel a sense of responsibility and determination, pushing you to be more organized and committed. This cosmic aspect is an excellent time to tackle tasks that require patience and perseverance, as the Capricorn energy lends itself well to handling challenges with a steady and structured mindset.

6 Wednesday

Mars ingress Libra. You might find yourself seeking harmony and cooperation in your interactions with others, valuing compromise and diplomacy over confrontation. This period can be an opportunity to improve your relationships and find common ground. It's a time to be more conscious of how your actions affect others and to seek win-win solutions. Embrace the energy of Mars in Libra as it guides collaborative ways of dealing with challenges and pursuing your goals.

7 Thursday

In the cosmic script of work objectives, the astrological landscape weaves a narrative of practical influence and potential. The celestial signatures inscribed in the cosmic canvas suggest a story of strategic growth and practical nuances within your career. Allow the astrological landscape to guide your practical actions in your professional journey, inviting you to navigate harmoniously with the celestial threads that shape your career narrative.

8 Friday

Moon ingress Aquarius. Mars trine Uranus. Your intuition heightens, and you can receive sudden insights that guide you toward fresh perspectives. Embrace the electric energy of Mars trine Uranus as it propels you forward on a path of exploration and self-discovery. Embracing your authentic self and staying open to unexpected possibilities can lead to exciting and transformative experiences during this cosmic alignment.

9 Saturday

With Mars opposing Saturn and Neptune while also experiencing a Full Moon, you might find yourself in a complex and challenging emotional landscape. This combination can bring up feelings of frustration, obstacles, and uncertainties. It's essential to navigate these energies with patience and careful consideration. The Mars-Saturn opposition may create tension and resistance, leading you to encounter roadblocks or limitations in pursuing your goals.

10 Sunday

With the Moon moving into Pisces and Mars forming a harmonious trine with Pluto, you may experience a surge of emotions and deep inner strength. This combination can fuel your passions and desires, propelling you towards transformative experiences. You might find that your intuition guides you toward the most authentic path. Trusting your instincts and embracing your emotions will enable you to make meaningful connections and forge deeper bonds with others.

11 Monday

With Mercury turning direct, you may feel a sense of relief and clarity after a period of introspection and reevaluation. During its retrograde phase, you might have faced communication hiccups and experienced delays in making decisions. As Mercury resumes its forward motion, you can expect matters to flow more smoothly. It's a favorable time to tie up loose ends, resolve misunderstandings, and move forward with your plans and projects.

12 Tuesday

As the Moon enters Aries, you may feel a surge of assertiveness and enthusiasm. It's a great time to take the initiative, pursue your goals passionately, and assert your individuality. Combining these aspects offers a potent blend of stability, optimism, and assertiveness, allowing you to make significant strides and create positive changes in various areas of your life. Trust your instincts, embrace new possibilities, and maximize this energetic, empowering cosmic alignment.

13 Wednesday

Celestial cues for career transitions and planning hint at subtle shifts and practical potential. These cosmic indications suggest a narrative of growth and evolution in your professional pursuits and strategic planning. The cosmic alignment prompts a rhythmic flow of sensible planning and visionary thinking. Engage with the nuanced interplay of celestial forces in your career, approaching tasks with heightened awareness for effective strategic outcomes.

14 Thursday

With the Moon's ingress into Taurus, you might notice a shift towards a more grounded and stable emotional state. This transit encourages you to find comfort in simple pleasures and focus on creating a sense of security and stability. You may seek activities that nourish your feelings, such as spending time in nature, enjoying good food, or engaging in creative pursuits. Taurus energy reminds you to slow down, savor the moment, and indulge in self-care.

15 Friday

With Mercury sextile Mars, you may be brimming with mental energy and assertiveness. This aspect brings a dynamic and quick-witted communication style, making it an excellent time for effectively expressing your ideas and persuading others. You will likely be more proactive in pursuing your goals and may find it easier to make decisions and take action. Your mind is sharp and focused, allowing you to tackle challenges with confidence and enthusiasm.

16 Saturday

The Moon in Gemini sees your emotional focus shift toward curiosity, communication, and social interactions. You may seek variety and mental stimulation, eager to engage in conversations and gather information. It is when your mind is sharp, adaptable, and open to new ideas. You might connect with others and share your thoughts and experiences. It's a favorable period for networking, learning, and exploring different perspectives.

17 Sunday

Within the harmonious cosmic frequencies in your familial haven, a suggestion emerges, inviting you to cultivate a balanced and nurturing atmosphere. This cosmic alignment encourages a rhythmic flow of family bonds and shared experiences. Embrace the nuanced interplay of celestial forces within your home, navigating your daily interactions with a heightened awareness of the harmonious dance orchestrating the cosmic symphony in your domestic life.

18 Monday

When Mercury forms a sextile aspect with Mars, you may notice a boost in your communication skills and mental agility. Your thoughts and ideas flow effortlessly, allowing you to express yourself assertively and precisely. During the Moon's ingress into Cancer, you might experience heightened emotions and more vital empathy. This period can be a time of increased sensitivity and nurturing tendencies, drawing you towards home and family matters.

19 Tuesday

Under subtle cosmic influence on creative projects, there's a suggestion of practical shifts and innovative thinking. The celestial alignment encourages infusing authenticity into professional pursuits, fostering a grounded yet creative atmosphere. Embrace transformative energies for practical breakthroughs and a strategic approach to creative endeavors. These cosmic hints suggest a narrative of growth and evolution in your professional pursuits and strategic planning.

20 Wednesday

As the Moon enters Leo, you may notice a shift in your emotional landscape. Your feelings become more expressive and vibrant, creating a flair for drama and creativity. This lunar transit encourages you to embrace your inner lion and bask in the spotlight, seeking recognition and validation for your unique qualities and talents. You might find yourself naturally drawn to activities that allow you to shine and showcase your individuality.

21 Thursday

Aligning cosmic energies for work efficiency, practical shifts, and productivity improvements are suggested. The celestial landscape encourages a straightforward approach to tasks, embracing transformative elements for a streamlined work routine. Leverage the cosmic currents for strategic planning, guiding you towards tangible career growth. This celestial alignment fosters a rhythmic flow of practical thinking and visionary planning.

22 Friday

As the Sun enters Virgo, you may sense a shift in your focus and approach to life. Your attention turns towards detail-oriented tasks and practical matters. This Virgo influence encourages you to analyze situations more critically, seeking efficiency and organization in your daily routines. You might feel a stronger desire to improve yourself and your surroundings, setting realistic goals and working diligently to achieve them.

23 Saturday

Virgo's analytical and practical energy can assist you in planning and strategizing your goals, ensuring they are both achievable and fulfilling. Take advantage of this lunar phase to establish healthy routines and habits and nurture your well-being. Embrace the powerful potential of the New Moon in Virgo to sow the seeds of growth and progress in various aspects of your life. Trust in the power of the New Moon to inspire new beginnings and set your intentions for the path ahead.

24 Sunday

As the Sun forms a square aspect with Uranus, you may experience a sense of restlessness and unpredictability. This cosmic alignment could bring about unexpected changes or disruptions, urging you to break free from routines and embrace a more unconventional approach to various aspects of your existence. You might feel an intense desire for independence and freedom, leading you to rebel against constraints and seek new and exciting experiences.

25 Monday

With the Moon's ingress into Libra and Venus moving into Leo, you may feel a shift in your emotional landscape and romantic inclinations. The Moon in Libra brings a heightened sense of harmony and a desire for balance in your relationships. You may seek companionship and cooperation, valuing diplomacy and compromise in your interactions with others. On the other hand, Venus in Leo adds a touch of drama and passion to your love life and personal expression.

26 Tuesday

With Venus forming harmonious trines to Saturn and Neptune and a sextile to Uranus, you experience stability, excitement, and dreaminess in your relationships and emotional experiences. The trine to Saturn brings a sense of maturity and commitment to your connections, allowing you to build strong foundations based on trust and loyalty. Simultaneously, the sextile to Uranus infuses a touch of novelty, adding excitement to social interactions.

27 Wednesday

With Venus opposing Pluto, you may experience intense emotions and power struggles in your relationships. This astrological aspect can bring underlying issues and hidden dynamics to the surface, demanding your attention and honesty. You might find yourself drawn to complex and passionate connections, but be cautious of any tendencies towards possessiveness. Focus on understanding the deeper layers of desires and motivations.

28 Thursday

With the Moon's ingress into Scorpio, you may experience a shift in your emotional landscape. Scorpio's influence brings intensity and depth to your feelings, encouraging you to delve into your innermost thoughts and desires. You might introspect and seek more significant meaning in your experiences during this time. Emotions could run more than usual, and you may be more inclined to keep your feelings private, guarding them like a secret.

29 Friday

With Uranus forming a sextile aspect to Neptune, you may experience a period of heightened creativity and inspiration. This astrological alignment sparks your imagination and encourages you to think outside the box, exploring innovative ideas and concepts. It's a time when your intuition and psychic sensitivity may be more pronounced, allowing you to tap into higher realms of consciousness and gain deeper insights into life's mysteries.

30 Saturday

As the Moon enters Sagittarius, you may feel a surge of optimism and a desire for adventure and expansion. This lunar transit brings a sense of freedom and openness to your emotions, inspiring you to seek new experiences and broaden your horizons. Sagittarius' influence encourages you to embrace a more adventurous and philosophical approach to life, enabling you to explore different cultures, belief systems, or educational opportunities.

31 Sunday

Within the cosmic script of your social sphere, the astrological landscape weaves a narrative of influence and potential. The celestial signatures inscribed in the cosmic canvas suggest a story of harmony and cosmic nuances within your social connections. Embrace the unfolding tale written in the stars, allowing the astrological landscape to guide your interpretations and actions in your social journey, inviting you to dance with the threads that shape your social narrative.

SEPTEMBER

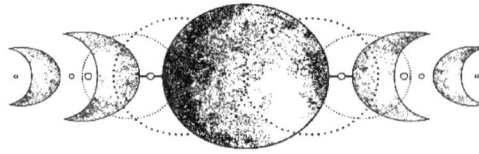

MOON MAGIC

Sun	Mon	Tue	Wed	Thu	Fri	Sat
	1	2	3	4	5	6
7	8	9	10	11	12	13
14	15	16	17	18	19	20
21	22	23	24	25	26	27
28	29	30				

NEW MOON

CORN/HARVEST MOON

1 Monday

Saturn in Pisces encourages you to confront any subconscious fears or limitations holding you back and embrace a more fluid and adaptable perspective. Saturn's influence in Pisces enables you to face unresolved emotional issues and work towards healing and letting go of past wounds. Embrace the lessons of this transit, as it can lead to a greater sense of connection with your emotions and a heightened awareness of the interconnectedness of all things.

2 Tuesday

The Capricorn Moon brings a disciplined and ambitious energy, encouraging you to set clear goals and work diligently towards achieving them. This transit is an excellent time to prioritize your responsibilities and make steady progress in your endeavors. Mercury's ingress into Virgo enhances your communication skills and attention to detail, making it easier to articulate your thoughts and analyze information effectively.

3 Wednesday

Mercury square Uranus. Embrace this transit's creative and innovative energy, allowing yourself to explore unique solutions and think outside the box. However, be mindful of the potential for impatience and be prepared to adapt to unexpected changes that may arise. Use this time to embrace the dynamic energy of Mercury square Uranus and harness it to your advantage, as it can lead to exciting discoveries and perspectives if you remain flexible and receptive.

4 Thursday

As the Moon enters Aquarius, you may experience a shift in your emotional landscape, characterized by a stronger desire for independence and a focus on collective connections. Aquarius' influence encourages you to embrace uniqueness and express your individuality more freely. You might be attracted to social causes and group activities promoting unity and progress during this lunar transition.

5 Friday

Mars square Jupiter. Use this energy to focus on your long-term goals and work towards them with a balanced approach rather than getting caught up in short-term gratification. Embrace the challenges presented by this aspect as opportunities for growth and self-awareness, allowing you to harness the dynamic energy of Mars and the expansive nature of Jupiter in a more controlled and purposeful manner.

6 Saturday

Uranus turns retrograde astrological event prompts you to review and reassess the changes and innovations unfolding in your life. It's a time to reflect on your desire for personal freedom and independence and to contemplate any areas where you may need to break free from limiting patterns or situations. Concurrently, with the Moon's ingress into Pisces, your emotions may become more intuitive and compassionate.

7 Sunday

During a Full Moon, you may feel the culmination of emotions and energies building up during the lunar cycle. This phase marks a time of heightened intensity and illumination, as the Sun and Moon oppose each other, creating a contrast between conscious and unconscious aspects of yourself. It's a moment for self-reflection and gaining clarity. Emotions may run high, and you might experience heightened sensitivity and a desire for release and transformation.

8 Monday

As the Moon enters Aries, you might feel a surge of assertiveness and a strong desire for action and independence. Aries' influence brings bold and dynamic energy to your emotions, motivating you to take the lead and initiate new ventures. During this lunar transit, you may be more inclined to express your feelings openly and directly without holding back. It's a favorable time to set clear intentions and pursue your goals with passion and determination.

9 Tuesday

In the visionary eleventh house, your Virgo Sun aligns with a desire for practical and tangible contributions to your social circles and community. Your analytical mind is directed toward collective goals, and you may find joy in organizing and optimizing shared projects. Friendships are essential to you, and you often connect with others through shared interests and a mutual commitment to improvement. Embrace the balance between practicality and innovation.

10 Wednesday

The Taurus Moon enhances your appreciation for the finer things in life, prompting you to seek beauty and harmony in your environment. It is an excellent time to nurture yourself, focus on self-care, and cultivate patience and perseverance in your endeavors. It is a favorable time to focus on growing peace and contentment. Embrace the steady and reliable energy of the Taurus Moon to find a sense of stability and joy in your emotional landscape.

11 Thursday

Subtle energies prompt you to bring purpose and clarity to your professional pursuits. Aligning cosmic forces in your creative workspace, there's a practical hint of change and innovation in the air. The celestial alignment prompts a down-to-earth approach to infuse your professional endeavors with new ideas. Embrace the current energies, allowing them to guide you towards straightforward creative breakthroughs and a pragmatic alignment with your career path.

12 Friday

With the Sun forming a harmonious sextile to Jupiter, you may experience a boost of optimism and confidence, allowing you to see the bigger picture and explore new opportunities with a positive mindset. As the Moon moves into Gemini, your emotional state may become more adaptable and curious, stimulating your desire for intellectual pursuits and social interactions. It is a favorable time to engage in meaningful conversations and connect with others on a deeper level.

13 Saturday

The Sun is conjunct with Mercury; you may experience mental clarity and self-expression. Your thoughts and ideas align seamlessly with your core identity, making it easier to communicate authentically. This astrological alignment enhances your communication skills and intellectual abilities, allowing you to articulate your thoughts with confidence and charisma. It's a favorable time for engaging in discussions, making presentations, or sharing your creative work.

14 Sunday

Within the cosmic script, the astrological landscape weaves a narrative of influence and potential. The celestial signatures inscribed in the cosmic canvas suggest a story of balanced growth and cosmic nuances within your leisure time. Embrace the unfolding tale written in the heavenly language, allowing the astrological landscape to guide your interpretations and actions, inviting you to dance harmoniously with the celestial threads that shape your weekend narrative.

15 Monday

Moon ingress Cancer. Cancer's influence brings a nurturing and empathetic energy, encouraging you to seek solace in the warmth of home and the embrace of loved ones. During this lunar transition, you might find yourself more attuned to your feelings and the emotions of those around you. It's a favorable time to focus on self-care and emotional well-being, allowing yourself to process unresolved emotions and find healing through introspection.

16 Tuesday

When Venus forms a sextile aspect to Mars, you may experience a harmonious blend of feminine and masculine energies within you. This astrological alignment enhances your social interactions and romantic pursuits, making it an ideal time for connecting with others emotionally and physically. The Venus-Mars sextile can also ignite passion and creative sparks in your relationships, allowing for greater intimacy and mutual understanding.

17 Wednesday

As the Moon moves into Leo, you may experience a surge of confidence and a desire to express yourself more boldly. This lunar transit fosters creativity and playfulness, encouraging you to seek recognition and appreciation for your unique qualities. However, with Mercury opposed to Saturn, you may also encounter challenges in communication and decision-making. Your thoughts may feel more focused on practical matters.

18 Thursday

As Mercury moves into Libra, you may seek greater harmony and balance in your communication style. This astrological influence encourages you to weigh different viewpoints and consider the perspectives of others in your interactions. However, with Mercury opposed to Neptune, there's a potential for miscommunication and confusion. You might encounter challenges in expressing your thoughts clearly, and there could be a tendency for misunderstandings.

19 Friday

With Mercury forming trines to Uranus and Pluto, your mental faculties are heightened, and you may experience a surge of insightful and transformative thinking. This astrological combination empowers you to grasp innovative ideas and delve into deep psychological realms quickly. Your thoughts are original and penetrating, making it an excellent time for problem-solving and creative endeavors as your focus shifts toward practicality and attention to detail.

20 Saturday

The Venus-Uranus square can inspire you to break free from old patterns and embrace your individuality. Still, finding a balance between seeking novelty and maintaining stability in your emotional connections is essential. While the square aspect can create tension, it offers growth and liberation opportunities. Use this period to authentically explore your desires and values, allowing yourself to evolve within your relationships while staying true to your core principles.

21 Sunday

As the Sun opposes Saturn, you may experience a sense of resistance and obstacles. This astrological aspect can bring a feeling of self-doubt or limitations, making it challenging to pursue goals. However, with the New Moon and the Moon's ingress into Libra, there is an opportunity for fresh starts. The New Moon offers a chance to set new intentions and plant seeds of growth, while the Moon in Libra fosters a desire for harmony and cooperation in your relationships.

22 Monday

As Mars moves into Scorpio, you may experience a shift in your energy and motivation. This astrological transit intensifies your drive and determination, making you more focused on your goals and desires. It's a time to delve deep into your passions and embrace your inner strength. Alongside the September Equinox, you may also feel balance and harmony. This seasonal shift offers renewal and reflection opportunities as the day and night become equal in length.

23 Tuesday

Sun opposed Neptune. Staying grounded and avoiding making important choices based solely on emotions or romantic notions is essential. This opposition can also enhance your empathy and imagination, allowing creative and spiritual exploration. However, be cautious of any tendencies towards self-deception or being overly trusting of others. Embrace the opportunity for introspection and inner growth, and strive for clarity and discernment to navigate with insight.

24 Wednesday

Sun trine Uranus astrological alignment enhances your ability to tap into your inner power and confidently embrace change. Your sense of individuality and uniqueness is rising, making it an ideal time to express your authentic self and explore innovative ideas. As the Moon moves into Scorpio, your emotions become more intense and focused, and you may find yourself drawn to more profound, transformative experiences.

25 Thursday

The Sun's radiant presence in your sector of self-discovery illuminates the cosmic path to personal empowerment. Bask in the solar glow as the celestial spotlight reveals the contours of your inner landscape. Under the solar rays, embark on a cosmic quest of self-awareness, where the journey within becomes a radiant pilgrimage toward the realization of your celestial potential. Feel the solar currents guide you through the phases of personal growth.

26 Friday

Sagittarius' influence encourages you to embrace freedom and independence, urging you to abandon the usual routine as you crave spontaneity. You might seek cultural activities that allow you to immerse yourself in different perspectives and beliefs. Use this time to tap into your adventurous spirit and explore the world with a curious and adventurous heart. Let the Sagittarius Moon inspire you to embrace new opportunities and seek inspiration in life's vast possibilities.

27 Saturday

The North Node's celestial compass directs your focus toward collective endeavors and social contributions. Trust the cosmic guidance as it leads you to participate in the grand tapestry of humanity's evolution. In the heavenly fellowship, follow the North Node's beacon towards meaningful connections and shared endeavors, contributing to the celestial symphony that uplifts the collective consciousness.

28 Sunday

With the luminous moon gracing your partnership sector, the cosmic ballad of love and connection takes center stage. Feel the tender melodies of emotional reciprocity and intimate harmony resonate through the celestial amphitheater of your relationships. The lunar glow illuminates the intricacies of your partnerships, inviting you to dance with the cosmic rhythms of empathy and understanding. Your abode transforms into a sanctuary where familial bonds bring tribulations.

OCTOBER

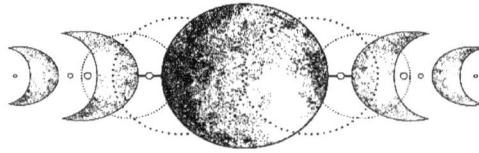

MOON MAGIC

Sun	Mon	Tue	Wed	Thu	Fri	Sat
			1	2	3	4
5	6	7	8	9	10	11
12	13	14	15	16	17	18
19	20	21	22	23	24	25
26	27	28	29	30	31	

New Moon

Hunters Moon

29 Monday

Moon ingress Capricorn astrological influence encourages you to focus on your responsibilities and long-term ambitions. Your emotions become more disciplined and determined, urging you to work diligently towards your objectives. Capricorn's energy fosters a sense of self-control and a willingness to take on challenges with perseverance. This transit is an excellent time to set clear boundaries and prioritize your tasks, ensuring you stay focused and organized.

30 Tuesday

A more stable landscape helps you channel your energy into a meaningful journey forward. A purposeful push towards developing new goals paves the way toward progress and increasing possibility in your life. Manifesting happiness is on the agenda; it cracks open a journey of kinship and companionship that bodes well for your romantic life. Being available to all that life can offer brings improvement ahead.

1 Wednesday

With the Moon moving into Aquarius, you may experience a heightened sense of individuality and a desire for innovation and social connection. This astrological influence encourages embracing uniqueness and engaging with a broader community. However, the Mercury square Jupiter aspect can lead to overconfidence or exaggeration in your communication. It's essential to be mindful of the potential for information overload.

2 Thursday

Life brings opportunities to shift your focus toward growth and advancement. Improvement ahead boosts confidence and brings lighter energy. It promotes a time that nurtures well-being and harmony in your life. As you improve your bottom line, you step out on a journey that offers a social connection. It brings the right environment to share with friends engagingly. A new realm of options in your life draws dividends.

3 Friday

Embrace the cosmic ambiance of your upcoming weekend activities as subtle energies beckon you to infuse your leisure moments with joy and simplicity. The celestial dance invites you to immerse yourself in the inspired vibrations that surround your weekend plans. Embrace the harmonious dance of cosmic forces within your downtime, allowing their relaxed touch to guide you towards moments of leisure and rejuvenation.

4 Saturday

Moon ingress Pisces. During this lunar transit, you might find solace in quiet reflection and creative pursuits that allow you to escape the demands of the everyday. It is an ideal time to offer your support and kindness, as the Pisces Moon enhances your ability to understand and relate to the feelings of others. Embrace the gentle and intuitive energy of the Pisces Moon to foster a sense of inner peace and forge meaningful connections that transcend words and logic.

5 Sunday

With the Sun illuminating your twelfth house, your Libra energy takes on a more reflective and spiritual quality. You may find a sense of balance and peace through solitude and introspection. Your diplomatic nature is turned inward as you seek harmony within the depths of your subconscious. Be mindful of the tendency to maintain peace and explore avenues of self-discovery and healing to achieve a more profound sense of balance and serenity.

6 Monday

Moon ingress Aries. Mercury ingress Scorpio. Combining Aries' boldness and Scorpio's depth can create a dynamic blend, motivating you to explore new horizons and engage in conversations beyond the surface. Embrace this energetic synergy to express yourself authentically and fearlessly while using the Scorpio influence to uncover insights and connect more profoundly with yourself and others.

7 Tuesday

Full Moon. Mercury square Pluto. During a Full Moon, you may experience heightened emotions and a sense of culmination. This astrological phase brings to light what is overlooked, offering a time of clarity and realization. However, Mercury square Pluto has the potential for intense and sometimes aggressive communication. It's essential to be cautious of power struggles and avoid using manipulation or control in your interactions.

8 Wednesday

As the Moon moves into Taurus, you may experience a sense of stability and a desire for comfort. This astrological influence encourages you to enjoy simple pleasures and sensory experiences. With Venus forming a sextile to Jupiter, this is a period of heightened positivity and harmony in your relationships. You might feel a stronger connection to your loved ones and a greater appreciation for the beauty around you.

9 Thursday

An opportunity is coming up for you that will be a good fit for your life. As you step out on a journey of increasing possibilities, life becomes lighter and sweeter. A creative venture becomes a hot topic of conversation in your circle of friends. It activates a group environment that nurtures your talents as you contribute knowledge and share your skills with others. It brings an enterprising time that keeps you on your toes.

10 Friday

Moon ingress Gemini. You may find your thoughts becoming more agile and adaptable, allowing you to explore various topics and perspectives. This lunar transit also enhances your social interactions, making it a favorable period for networking and making new connections. Embrace the Gemini Moon's energy to expand your knowledge and engage in lively exchanges while fostering a sense of lightness and playfulness in your interactions with others.

11 Saturday

Venus opposed Saturn's astrological aspect, which can bring a sense of limitation and a need to confront any insecurities or fears hindering your ability to connect with others. You might feel a sense of distance or coldness in your interactions, leading to potential conflicts or feelings of isolation. It's essential to approach this opposition with patience and a willingness to address any underlying issues honestly and sensitively.

12 Sunday

As the Moon moves into Cancer, you may notice a shift towards heightened emotional sensitivity and a desire for comfort and security. This astrological influence encourages you to connect with your feelings deeper and seek solace in familiar surroundings. Cancer's energy fosters a nurturing and compassionate atmosphere, making it an ideal time to spend quality moments with loved ones and engage in self-care practices that nourish your soul.

13 Monday

As Venus moves into Libra, you may focus more on relationships and harmony. This astrological shift encourages you to seek balance and cooperation in your interactions with others. Libra's energy fosters a desire for fairness and mutual understanding, making it an ideal time to strengthen connections and resolve conflicts through open communication. You might find yourself drawn to beauty and aesthetics, with an appreciation for art and culture.

14 Tuesday

As the Moon moves into Leo, your emotions become more expressive and enthusiastic, urging you to seek recognition and creative outlets. Venus forming trines to Uranus and Pluto offers exciting and transformative shifts in your relationships and creative pursuits. It can inspire you to embrace innovation and explore your passions with a newfound intensity. This combination encourages you to infuse your connections and self-expression with authenticity and depth.

15 Wednesday

Within the cosmic script of your professional aspirations, the astrological landscape weaves a narrative of influence and potential. The celestial signatures inscribed in the cosmic canvas suggest a story of strategic growth and cosmic nuances within your career. Embrace the unfolding tale written in the heavenly language, allowing the astrological landscape to guide your interpretations and actions in your professional journey, inviting you to shape your career narrative.

16 Thursday

With the Moon moving into Virgo, you may feel a heightened sense of organization and attention to detail. This astrological transition encourages you to focus on practical matters and tasks that require precision. Virgo's energy fosters a desire for efficiency and a willingness to tackle responsibilities head-on. During this lunar transit, you might find satisfaction in decluttering, organizing your space, or engaging in activities that contribute to your well-being.

17 Friday

When the Sun is square Jupiter, you may experience heightened enthusiasm and optimism, but it's essential to be mindful of potential excesses. This astrological aspect can bring a sense of expansiveness and a desire to take on more than you can handle. While this energy can boost your confidence and creativity, there's a risk of overestimating your capabilities or over-committing. Find a balance between your ambitions and a realistic, achievable assessment.

18 Saturday

As Saturn takes residence in your home and family sector, the celestial architect lays the foundation for stability and structure within your domestic realm. Witness the astral mason at work, constructing pillars of responsibility and discipline. Under Saturn's cosmic blueprint, your abode transforms into a sanctuary of resilience, a celestial fortress where familial bonds withstand the tests of time and cosmic tribulations.

19 Sunday

Moon ingress Libra lunar transit, you might find yourself more attuned to the needs and feelings of those around you, making it a favorable time for open conversations. The Libra Moon also enhances your appreciation for art, beauty, and aesthetics, prompting you to engage in activities that bring joy and a sense of refinement. Embrace this lunar energy to foster meaningful connections, create a peaceful atmosphere, and express your emotions gracefully and carefully.

20 Monday

Mercury conjunct Mars astrological alignment can bring a sense of urgency to your thoughts and communication style. Your mind becomes more quick-witted and proactive, encouraging you to express your ideas with confidence and passion. This conjunction can also enhance your ability to make decisions swiftly, but it's essential to be mindful of impulsive reactions or rushing into situations without considering all angles.

21 Tuesday

During a New Moon, you may experience a fresh start and a sense of new beginnings. This astrological phase marks a time of planting seeds for future growth and setting intentions for the upcoming cycle. As the Moon moves into Scorpio, your emotions may become more intense and introspective. Scorpio's energy encourages you to delve deep into your feelings and explore the hidden aspects of your inner world. This lunar transit fosters a desire for transformation and personal evolution.

22 Wednesday

Neptune ingress Pisces astrological shift encourages you to explore your inner world with compassion and sensitivity. Pisces' energy fosters a merging of boundaries and a desire to dissolve barriers between yourself and others. During this transit, you might find yourself more attuned to the subtle energies around you, engaging in creative and artistic pursuits that allow you to express your emotions and connect with the intangible.

23 Thursday

As the Sun moves into Scorpio, you may sense a shift towards intensity and a desire for deeper understanding. This astrological transition encourages you to explore the hidden layers of your emotions and the mysteries of life. Scorpio's energy fosters a sense of empowerment and a willingness to confront the truths beneath the surface. You might feel drawn to introspection and self-discovery, seeking transformation and growth during this period.

24 Friday

As the Moon moves into Sagittarius, you might feel a sense of adventurous optimism and a desire for exploration. This astrological shift encourages you to broaden your horizons and seek new experiences. However, with the Sun square Pluto, you may also encounter a period of inner transformation and potential power struggles. This aspect can bring challenges that prompt you to confront deep-seated issues and release what no longer serves you.

25 Saturday

When Mercury forms a trine aspect to Saturn, you may experience a period of enhanced focus and practical thinking. This astrological alignment empowers you with a disciplined and systematic mindset, making it an excellent time for planning, organizing, and tackling tasks that require attention to detail. Your communication becomes more precise and thoughtful, allowing you to convey your ideas and opinions with clarity and authority.

26 Sunday

Moon ingress Capricorn astrological transition encourages you to prioritize responsibilities and focus on tasks that require diligence and determination. Capricorn's energy fosters a desire for practicality and structure, making it an ideal time to set clear objectives and work towards achieving them. During this lunar transition, you might find satisfaction in accomplishing tasks and taking steps toward your long-term ambitions.

27 Monday

Life is ripe with potential and ready to blossom. It brings choices and decisions that promote rapid expansion as you shift your focus toward developing your career path. Mapping out long-term goals becomes a turning point that enables you to chase your vision and gain traction on improving circumstances. It lets you use your talents to stunning effect as you head towards change. It is a time that offers opportunities for growth and expansion.

28 Tuesday

Mars trines Jupiter. This trine enhances your ability to overcome obstacles while fostering a spirit of generosity and a willingness to help. Embrace the Mars-Jupiter trine's energy to channel your passion and vitality into fulfilling endeavors. Your drive becomes fueled by a desire for growth and expansion, making it a favorable time to embark on new ventures. Use this cosmic synergy to reach for the stars and make the most of the opportunities that come your way.

29 Wednesday

The Mars trine Saturn aspect empowers you with disciplined energy and a practical approach to your actions. However, Mercury's opposition to Uranus can bring sudden shifts in your thinking and potential disruptions in your plans. Embrace the Aquarius Moon's energy to embrace your individuality, allow the Mercury-Neptune trine to inspire imaginative thinking, and use the Mars-Saturn trine to work diligently towards your goals.

30 Thursday

With Mercury forming a sextile to Pluto, you may experience a period of deep insights and assertive communication. This astrological alignment enhances your ability to delve into profound subjects and uncover hidden truths. Your thoughts become more penetrating, and your conversations carry a transformative energy. This sextile encourages you to engage in meaningful discussions and seek information that can lead to personal growth and understanding.

November

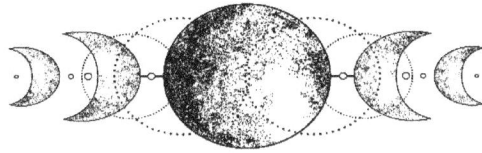

MOON MAGIC

Sun	Mon	Tue	Wed	Thu	Fri	Sat
						1
2	3	4	5	6	7	8
9	10	11	12	13	14	15
16	17	18	19	20	21	22
23	24	25	26	27	28	29
30						

NEW MOON

BEAVER MOON

31 Friday

During the Moon ingress Pisces lunar transit, you might find solace in artistic or creative activities that allow you to express your emotions. It is also a time when you may feel more attuned to spiritual matters and seek moments of quiet introspection. Embrace the Pisces Moon's energy to nurture your emotional well-being, engage with your creativity, and tap into the subtler dimensions of life that bring you peace and fulfillment.

1 Saturday

Within the celestial script of your social connections, the astrological landscape weaves a narrative of influence and potential. The divine signatures inscribed in the cosmic canvas suggest a story of harmony and cosmic nuances within your social bonds. Allow the astrological landscape to guide your interpretations and actions in your social journey, inviting you to dance harmoniously with the celestial threads that shape your social narrative.

2 Sunday

As the Moon moves into Aries, you may experience a surge of energy and assertiveness. This astrological shift encourages you to take the initiative and approach your emotions with a sense of enthusiasm. However, with Venus square Jupiter, there's potential for indulgence and excess in matters of the heart. This aspect can bring a desire for pleasure and enjoyment, but it's important to exercise moderation and avoid overextending yourself.

3 Monday

Celestial configurations hint at subtle shifts and transformative potential in your career landscape. These cosmic whispers suggest a narrative of growth and evolution in your professional pursuits and strategic planning. Engage with the hints presented by the celestial configurations, allowing their guidance to enhance your understanding and connection with the cosmic energies that shape your career path.

4 Tuesday

Mars trine Neptune astrological alignment empowers you to channel your energy into imaginative pursuits and connect with your dreams and ideals. As Mars moves into Sagittarius, your drive becomes fueled by a desire for exploration and adventure. This transition encourages you to take risks and expand your horizons. However, with the Moon moving into Taurus and Mars opposing Uranus, there's potential for disruptions and sudden changes in your emotions and plans.

5 Wednesday

Full Moon is a time of greater awareness of your inner desires and conflicts. The Full Moon encourages you to assess your progress and intentions since the New Moon, and it can serve as a reminder to release what no longer serves you. It's an ideal opportunity for self-reflection and adjustments to align with your goals. Embrace the energy of the Full Moon to bring matters to fruition, find clarity in your emotions, and embrace the potential for transformation and renewal.

6 Thursday

Mars sextile Pluto astrological alignment empowers you to channel your drive and passion into meaningful endeavors. As the Moon moves into Gemini, your emotions become more curious and adaptable. It is when you might seek out diverse experiences and engage in conversations stimulating your mind. With Venus entering Scorpio, your approach to love and relationships may take on a more intense and profound quality.

7 Friday

In the first house, your Scorpio Sun radiates intensity, making your personality magnetic. You approach life with a sense of purpose and transformation, often experiencing life events as opportunities for profound personal growth. Your passionate and resourceful nature may manifest in a solid drive to assert yourself and make a lasting impact. Embrace your transformative energy as a catalyst for positive change in your own life and the lives of those around you.

8 Saturday

With Uranus moving into Taurus, you may enter a period of revolutionary change and innovation in matters related to stability and resources. This astrological transition encourages you to embrace new ways of approaching material and financial issues. As Venus squares Pluto, there's potential for intense emotions and dynamics in relationships and desires. This aspect can lead to transformations in your connections and a need to address underlying issues.

9 Sunday

As Mercury turns retrograde, you may experience a period of introspection and review in your communication and thought processes. This astrological phenomenon can bring a sense of slowing down, which helps revisit matters. It's advisable to be cautious when making important decisions or signing contracts during this time, as misunderstandings and miscommunications could arise more easily.

10 Monday

With the Moon moving into Leo, you may notice a shift toward a more expressive and dynamic emotional state. This astrological transition encourages you to embrace individuality and seek opportunities to shine and be recognized. Leo's energy fosters a desire for creativity and a need for appreciation. During this lunar transit, you might find yourself drawn to activities that allow you to showcase your talents and receive positive attention.

11 Tuesday

Jupiter turns retrograde. While external growth might slow down temporarily, the Jupiter retrograde energy invites you to explore your inner world and broaden your perspective through self-discovery and spiritual exploration. Use this phase to delve into your philosophies and consider how to align your aspirations with your inner values better, embracing the Jupiter retrograde energy to cultivate inner wisdom and refine your expansion path.

12 Wednesday

Mercury conjunct Mars astrological alignment empowers you to express your thoughts and ideas boldly and confidently. Your mind becomes sharp and decisive, making it a favorable time for making decisions and taking swift action on your plans. As the Moon moves into Virgo, your emotions may align with a more practical and analytical approach. This combination encourages you to focus on details and engage in tasks that require precision and organization.

13 Thursday

You crack the code to a bright chapter when revealing information that opens up prospects. It offers a lush environment from which to chase developing dreams. It links you with kindred spirits, which draws heightened opportunities to mingle with your circle of friends. Something newsworthy filters down the gossip line, bringing new information to light. It attracts a happy time, deepening ties, and enjoying shared moments with friends.

14 Friday

Life lightens, bringing laughter, fun, and social engagement to the forefront of your life. It shines the spotlight on sharing with friends as invitations bring rising prospects into your life. It sets the stage to chase dreams and embrace connectedness as you touch down on a promising journey of developing meaningful bonds in your life. It creates space to nurture new dreams and goals as positive energy flows into your world.

15 Saturday

Moon ingress Libra astrological transition encourages you to seek balance and fairness in your interactions with others. Libra's energy fosters a desire for companionship and a willingness to find common ground. You might engage in activities promoting cooperation and diplomacy during this lunar transition. This ingress is a favorable time to engage in conversations that foster understanding and promote harmony.

16 Sunday

The celestial compass points you toward the path of personal evolution and spiritual growth. Trust the cosmic navigation as it directs you through the labyrinth of self-discovery. In the celestial unfolding of your destiny, follow this guiding light towards a higher plane of existence, where the cosmic dance of purpose harmonizes with the symphony of your soul. The astral winds whisper tales of higher knowledge, encouraging you to seek wisdom.

17 Monday

With the Moon moving into Scorpio, your emotions may become more intense and introspective. This combination encourages you to embrace transformation and delve into your inner world. Embrace the Sun's trines to Jupiter and Saturn's energies to find success through optimism and strategic planning. Let the Mercury-Pluto sextile inspire potent conversations, and allow the Scorpio Moon's influence to guide you in exploring your emotions during this dynamic period.

18 Tuesday

The Sun's radiant journey through your social sector bathes your connections in the golden glow of cosmic camaraderie. Revel in the warmth of communal bonds as the celestial spotlight shines on your social constellation. Under the solar radiance, forge connections that resonate with the harmonies of shared aspirations and collective joy, creating a stellar network that twinkles with the light of shared purpose.

19 Wednesday

Mercury ingress Scorpio astrological transition encourages you to explore deeper truths beneath the surface. However, with Mercury opposed to Uranus, your conversations have the potential for unexpected disruptions and unconventional thinking. This aspect can bring unique insights but also requires careful consideration. The Mercury trine Neptune aspect adds a touch of intuition and creativity to your thoughts and expression.

20 Thursday

The New Moon astrological phase marks a time of planting seeds for future growth. As the Sun conjoins Mercury, your thoughts and communication align with your core identity and goals. With Mercury moving into Sagittarius, your thinking expands to embrace broader perspectives and a thirst for knowledge. The Uranus sextile Neptune aspect adds a touch of innovation and creativity to your ideas, inspiring you to explore imaginative and progressive concepts.

21 Friday

As you navigate the tension of the Sun-Uranus opposition, allow the Sun-Neptune trine to guide you toward embracing your dreams and engaging in artistic or spiritual pursuits. This combination invites you to find a balance between the need for liberation and the desire for inner harmony and creativity. Embrace the influence of both aspects to navigate this period flexibly, embracing change while maintaining a connection to your inner vision.

22 Saturday

With the Sun moving into Sagittarius, you may experience a shift towards a more adventurous and open-minded energy. This astrological transition encourages you to embrace a broader perspective and seek new horizons. As Mercury forms a trine to Saturn, your communication becomes focused, allowing you to engage in productive conversations and practical thinking. With the Moon moving into Capricorn, your emotions may become more grounded and goal-oriented.

23 Sunday

With the Sun forming a sextile to Pluto, you may experience a period of empowerment and transformation. This astrological alignment empowers you with inner strength and a desire to delve deep into matters that require change and growth. This sextile encourages you to tap into your hidden resources and uncover hidden truths. It's a favorable time to make positive changes, harness your power, and embrace a greater sense of self-awareness.

24 Monday

You discover helpful options that create a golden triangle of possibility. It brings luck, improvement, and security. Gathering your resources, you are open to a time of learning and refinement that shines on your skills. It gets the ball rolling on upgrading your career path, letting you take advantage of incoming opportunities that offer rising prospects. Advancement is coming, bringing a fertile environment from which to grow your life.

25 Tuesday

Mercury conjunct Venus. Moon ingress Aquarius. This combination encourages you to embrace community and explore unconventional ideas. Embrace the Mercury-Venus conjunction's energy to foster meaningful connections and heartfelt conversations. Let the Aquarius Moon inspire you to think outside the box and engage with a broader perspective as you navigate this dynamic period with a blend of intellectual engagement and social openness.

26 Wednesday

With Venus forming trines to Jupiter and Saturn, you may experience a period of harmonious and balanced energies in matters of love, relationships, and creativity. This astrological alignment empowers you with optimism and stability in your emotional connections. The Venus Jupiter trine encourages the expansion of love and joy, while the Venus Saturn trine adds a practical and disciplined touch to your interactions.

27 Thursday

It's a favorable time to come together with loved ones and reflect on the blessings in your life. Your emotions may become more sensitive and attuned to the needs and feelings of others, making this holiday an excellent opportunity for acts of kindness and heartfelt expressions of appreciation. Embrace the Pisces Moon's energy to foster a sense of togetherness, share your love, and immerse yourself in Thanksgiving's warm and nurturing vibes.

28 Friday

As Saturn turns direct, you may feel a shift in the cosmic energies influencing your life. It often signifies a period of increased clarity and momentum in areas where you've been working diligently to establish order and achieve your goals. Saturn's direct motion often represents a time when long-term plans and ambitions can move more smoothly. It encourages you to continue taking responsible steps toward your aspirations, offering a sense of renewed determination and progress.

29 Saturday

As Mercury resumes its usual forward motion, you can expect smoother interactions and greater ease in conveying your thoughts and ideas. It's an excellent time to tie up loose ends, resolve any lingering issues, and move forward with plans and projects that may have been on hold during the retrograde phase. Embrace this shift as an opportunity to regain mental clarity and move ahead confidently in your decision-making and communication endeavors.

30 Sunday

Embrace the Aries Moon's energy to initiate new projects and confidently assert your needs while allowing the Venus-Uranus opposition to encourage adaptability. The Venus-Neptune trine inspires you to approach your connections with empathy and understanding, and the Venus-Sagittarius influence invites you to explore the world of love and values with curiosity and enthusiasm as you navigate this dynamic period.

DECEMBER

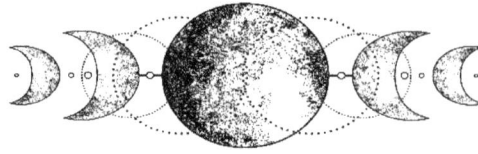

MOON MAGIC

Sun	Mon	Tue	Wed	Thu	Fri	Sat
	1	2	3	4	5	6
7	8	9	10	11	12	13
14	15	16	17	18	19	20
21	22	23	24	25	26	27
28	29	30	31			

New Moon

Cold Moon

DECEMBER

1 Monday

Opportunities in the workplace draw an active time that offers growth and prosperity. It opens your life to a broader bounty of possibility as an opportunity comes knocking, and this gives you an exciting sign that things are shifting forward in your life. Newfound motivation fuels inspiration and enables you to launch into a chapter of gain and progression. Life is ripe with remarkable possibilities worthy of development.

2 Tuesday

With the Moon moving into Taurus, you may notice a shift towards a more grounded and sensual emotional state. This astrological transition encourages you to seek comfort, stability, and a deeper connection to your physical senses. Taurus' energy fosters a desire for relaxation and enjoying life's simple pleasures. As Venus forms a sextile to Pluto, your relationships and passions may take on a more intense and transformative quality.

3 Wednesday

You head towards an extended time that reinvents the potential possible in your world. A transformational aspect has a profound effect on your spirit. It offers to heal and nurture well-being as you improve the foundations and nurture the possibilities in your world. It encourages you to push the barriers back and head towards change. A new role on offer inspires a great deal of excitement. The conditions for growth ripen, and you achieve more stability and progression.

4 Thursday

The Full Moon's illumination invites you to assess your progress and achievements since the previous New Moon, offering a chance to make adjustments and set intentions for the future. Embrace the Gemini Moon's energy to stimulate your curiosity and enhance communication while using the Full Moon's radiance to gain insights, find closure, and align emotions with intentions as you navigate this phase of heightened mental activity and emotional fulfillment.

5 Friday

Within the harmonious cosmic frequencies for a fluid day, there's a suggestion of adaptability and practicality in the air. This cosmic alignment encourages a rhythmic flow of flexible activities and a responsive approach. Embrace the nuanced interplay of celestial forces within your daily routine, navigating your tasks with a heightened awareness of the harmonious dance orchestrating the cosmic symphony throughout your day.

6 Saturday

With the Moon moving into Cancer, you may feel a deep emotional connection to your inner world and a desire for comfort and security. This astrological transition encourages you to nurture your emotional well-being and seek solace in the familiarity of home and family. Cancer's energy fosters a sense of empathy and sensitivity, making it an ideal time to connect with your feelings. As Mercury forms a trine to Neptune, your communication takes on an imaginative quality.

7 Sunday

Within the harmonious cosmic frequencies for a weekend escape, there's a suggestion of balance and enjoyment in the air. This cosmic alignment encourages a rhythmic flow of leisurely pursuits and relaxed moments. Embrace the nuanced interplay of celestial forces within your weekend agenda, navigating your day with a heightened awareness of the harmonious dance orchestrating the cosmic symphony in your leisurely moments.

8 Monday

There's a subtle suggestion of alignment and flow in the celestial forecast. The cosmic interplay invites you to harmonize with the vibrations surrounding your daily tasks. Navigate your day with a graceful dance of heavenly forces, allowing their rhythmic touch to guide you toward moments of effortless execution and progress. Embrace the harmonious dance of cosmic forces, allowing their invigorating touch to show moments of achievement and focused determination.

9 Tuesday

With Mars forming a square to Saturn, you may encounter potential frustration and obstacles in your pursuits. This astrological aspect can clash between your desires for action and the need for discipline and structure. You might find moving forward with your plans challenging, encountering delays or limitations that test your patience. While this can be frustrating, viewing these challenges as opportunities for growth and endurance is essential.

10 Wednesday

With the Moon moving into Virgo, you may feel more analytical and detail-oriented. This astrological transition encourages you to focus on practical matters and attend to the finer points of your daily life. Virgo's energy fosters a desire for order and efficiency. Additionally, with Neptune turning direct, you might experience greater clarity and inspiration in your creative and spiritual pursuits. This cosmic shift can bring a boost of imaginative and intuitive energy.

11 Thursday

Mercury trine Neptune astrological alignment empowers you to communicate and think more intuitively and empathetically. Your dreams and a desire for spiritual insight may influence your thoughts. As Mercury moves into Sagittarius, your thinking becomes more expansive and adventurous. This combination encourages you to explore new ideas and broaden your horizons through meaningful conversations and learning experiences.

12 Friday

As the Moon gracefully enters Libra, you may sense a gentle wave of balance and harmony washing over your emotions. This astrological transition encourages you to seek equilibrium in your interactions and surroundings. Libra's energy fosters a penchant for seeking compromise and beauty. You might crave moments of peace and appreciation for aesthetics. It's a time to embrace your inner diplomat and to foster connections with others through understanding and cooperation.

13 Saturday

With Mercury forming a sextile to Pluto, you might find your thoughts and communication taking on a more insightful quality. This astrological aspect empowers you to delve deep into matters, uncover hidden truths, and engage in meaningful conversations. It's as if a veil is lifted, allowing you to see beneath the surface of things. This cosmic alignment encourages you to express your ideas and thoughts with intensity and authenticity.

14 Sunday

Mars square Neptune's astrological aspect can bring about a clash between your drive to take decisive action and the nebulous influence of Neptune, which can cloud your motivations and goals. It's as if you're navigating through a foggy landscape, making it difficult to see the path ahead clearly. This cosmic alignment calls for caution and self-awareness, as impulsive actions or hasty decisions may lead to unintended consequences.

15 Monday

Moon ingress Scorpio astrological transition could deepen emotions and heighten the focus on your ambitions and long-term goals. The Scorpio Moon encourages you to delve into your innermost feelings, making it a favorable time for introspection and exploring matters of intimacy and transformation. With Mars in Capricorn, your actions become more calculated and driven by a desire for success and achievement.

16 Tuesday

The celestial signatures inscribed in the cosmic canvas suggest a story of efficiency and cosmic nuances within your daily routine. Embrace the unfolding tale written in the heavenly language, allowing the astrological landscape to guide your interpretations and actions throughout your workday, inviting you to dance harmoniously with the celestial threads that shape your daily narrative. These cosmic whispers suggest a narrative of clarity and focus throughout your workday.

17 Wednesday

Sun square Saturn. Moon ingress Sagittarius. Sagittarius' energy encourages you to seek new horizons and embrace a broader perspective. While the Sun-Saturn square may pose obstacles, it's essential to use this cosmic tension as an opportunity for personal growth and reassess your goals. The Sagittarius Moon's energy can inspire you to stay hopeful and open to new possibilities, even in adversity.

18 Thursday

Celestial configurations hint at subtle shifts and transformative potential in your daily landscape. These cosmic whispers suggest a narrative of growth and evolution throughout your day. Engage with the hints presented by the celestial configurations, allowing their guidance to enhance your understanding and connection with the cosmic energies that shape your daily plans. Allow the astrological landscape to guide your actions throughout your day.

19 Friday

The cosmic rhythm of your daily hustle beckons you to infuse your workday with purpose and determination. The celestial dance invites you to immerse yourself in the inspired vibrations that surround your daily agenda. Embrace the harmonious dance of cosmic forces within your routines, allowing their motivating touch to guide you toward moments of accomplishment and focus. News arrives that brings a focus on engaging with your social life.

20 Saturday

With the arrival of a New Moon, you're entering a phase of fresh beginnings and potential transformations. This astrological event marks a moment for setting intentions and initiating new projects. It's a time to plant seeds for the future and to focus on what you wish to manifest. As the Moon moves into Capricorn, you'll likely feel more discipline and practicality in your pursuits. Capricorn's energy encourages you to take a structured approach to achieving your ambitions.

21 Sunday

Sun square Neptune's astrological aspect can cast a veil of illusion or idealism over your ambitions, making it crucial to remain discerning in your pursuits. Additionally, Venus square Saturn may challenge relationships and matters of the heart, requiring patience and effort to overcome obstacles. However, as we celebrate the December Solstice and the Sun's shift into Capricorn, there's an opportunity for a fresh start and increased focus on practicality and responsibility.

22 Monday

Moon ingress Aquarius astrological transition encourages you to embrace individuality, unconventional ideas, and desire freedom. Aquarius' energy fosters a sense of community and a need to connect with like-minded individuals who share your ideals and aspirations. During this lunar transition, you might be drawn to social causes, innovative thinking, or unique experiences that allow you to express your authentic self.

23 Tuesday

Within the harmonious cosmic frequencies for a balanced day, there's a suggestion of equilibrium and practicality in the air. This cosmic alignment encourages a rhythmic flow of balanced activities and a steady pace. Embrace the nuanced interplay of celestial forces within your daily routine, navigating your tasks with a heightened awareness of the harmonious dance orchestrating the cosmic symphony throughout your workday.

24 Wednesday

With Venus forming a square to Neptune, you might find that matters of the heart and finances become hazy and uncertain. This astrological aspect can bring about idealistic or unrealistic perceptions of relationships and money matters. It's essential to exercise caution and avoid making significant decisions based solely on romantic notions or financial fantasies during this period. As Venus enters Capricorn, you'll notice a shift to a grounded approach to love and resources.

25 Thursday

As the Moon gracefully moves into Pisces on Christmas Day, you may experience a heightened empathy, spirituality, and emotional connection. This astrological transition infuses the holiday atmosphere with magic and compassion. Pisces' energy fosters a desire for unity, artistic expression, and a deep relation to the mystical aspects of life. You might find that the true spirit of Christmas shines through acts of kindness and a willingness to share with others.

26 Friday

The astrological landscape weaves a narrative of influence and potential. The celestial signatures inscribed in the cosmic canvas suggest a story of efficiency and cosmic nuances within your daily routine. Embrace the unfolding tale written in the heavenly language, allowing the astrological landscape to guide your interpretations and actions throughout your workday, inviting you to dance harmoniously to shape your daily narrative.

27 Saturday

As the Moon shifts into Aries, you might feel a surge of energy and assertiveness. This astrological transition encourages you to take the initiative and pursue your goals with a strong sense of determination. Aries' energy is dynamic and competitive, making it an excellent time to tackle challenges and start new projects with enthusiasm. During this lunar phase, you may be drawn to physical activities and outdoor adventures.

28 Sunday

Within the cosmic ambiance of your day's activities, subtle energies beckon you to infuse your leisure moments with joy and simplicity. The celestial dance invites you to immerse yourself in the inspired vibrations that surround your weekend plans. Embrace the harmonious dance of cosmic forces within your downtime, allowing their relaxed touch to guide you towards moments of leisure and rejuvenation.

29 Monday

As the Moon gracefully enters Taurus, you may notice a shift towards a more grounded and stable emotional state. This astrological transition encourages you to seek comfort and security in your surroundings and connect with the sensual pleasures of life. Taurus' energy fosters a desire for simplicity, routine, and a connection to the physical world. During this time, you might find solace in the simple joys of good food, soothing music, or the beauty of nature.

30 Tuesday

When Mercury squares Saturn, you may encounter challenges expressing your thoughts and ideas. You might struggle to communicate your thoughts effectively or face obstacles in communicating your message to others. This aspect can bring a sense of mental tension and may lead to self-doubt. It can also indicate a tendency to be overly critical of yourself or others, hindering your ability to connect and collaborate effectively.

31 Wednesday

On New Year's Eve, when the Moon enters Gemini, you'll likely feel a shift in your emotional energy and desire for variety and social interaction. This lunar placement encourages you to embrace curiosity, engage in stimulating conversations, and explore different interests and ideas. You may find yourself drawn to celebrations that involve lively gatherings, intellectual pursuits, or even short trips to satisfy your craving for novelty and mental stimulation.

1 Thursday

On New Year's Day, as Mercury ingresses into Capricorn and forms a challenging square with Neptune, you may encounter cognitive fog and confusion in your thoughts and communication. This aspect can make it difficult for you to express clearly and may lead to misunderstandings with others. Neptune's dreamy influence might cloud your typically sharp and practical thinking, causing you to second-guess your decisions and perceive reality through a more idealistic lens.

Astrology, Tarot & Horoscope Books.

Mystic Cat

Mystic Cat Tarot

In Relationship Reading
$15.00

Crossroads
$10.00

Next Relationship Reading
$15.00

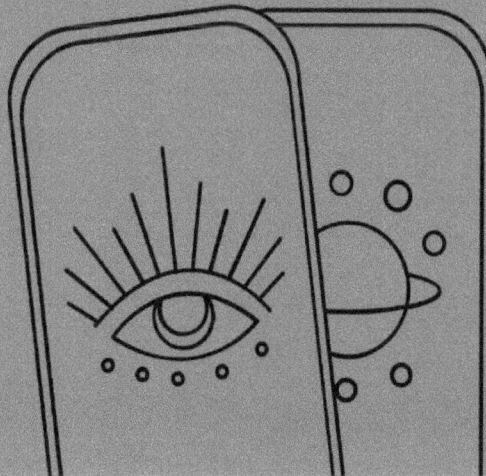

Ohoroscope@Hotmail.com